MONARCH®
NOTES AND STUDY GUIDES

COLLEGE LEVEL

HISTORY
OF EDUCATION

by
Leo Charles Daley
Department of Education
Jersey State College

Distributed by:

MONARCH PRESS, INC.
387 Park Avenue South
New York, N.Y. 10016

We would like to thank the numerous college professors throughout the country who have requested that this type of book be published to supplement the textbook used in their classes. The many helpful suggestions received from these teachers have assisted us in providing a well organized set of notes in this new edition which will give the student a proper understanding of the course by aiding him in the study of his textbook.

Library of Congress Catalog Card Number: 66-27225

CONTENTS

INTRODUCTION

VALUE OF
EDUCATIONAL HISTORY

EDUCATIONAL PROBLEMS. The problems of education derive from the following basic questions:

1. PURPOSE. What are *the purposes* of education?
2. DETERMINATION. How are these purposes *determined*?
3. SYSTEM. What is *the role of the educational system* in society?
4. SELECTION. *Who* should be educated?
5. CONTENT. What is the *correct content* for education?
6. EDUCATOR. What is the role of *the educator*?
7. LEARNER. What is the role of *the learner*?
8. METHOD. What are *the methods* of teaching?
9. VALUE. What is the conception of educational *value*?
10. CONTRIBUTION. What educational activities *contribute to the "good life"* of the individual? Of society?

PROBLEMS IN THE HISTORY OF EDUCATION. The historian of education considers the above questions in the light of historical developments. He considers such questions as:

1. EARLIER CIVILIZATIONS. How have *earlier civilizations* determined their educational goals?
2. GREAT THINKERS. What have *great thinkers* of the past theorized about educational aims and methods?
3. CURRICULUM. How has *the curriculum* developed through the ages?
4. STATUS. What was *the status* of teachers in past ages?
5. METHOD. How did *students learn* in earlier societies?
6. ROLE. What was *the role of the school* in earlier societies?
7. DEVELOPMENT OF THEORIES. What was *the development of theories of educational value*?

VALUE OF THE STUDY OF HISTORY. The student of educational history may achieve the following gains:

1. UNDERSTANDING PRESENT EDUCATIONAL PRACTICE. Modern educational practices did not arrive fully developed upon the social scene. The history of education helps one to understand the growth and development of these practices. It enables the student to realize how these practices came into existence.
2. KNOWLEDGE OF PROMINENT EDUCATORS. Many great thinkers of civilization evolved theories of education and have put those theories into practice in their own

5

societies. A knowledge of the lives and theories of these great educators will enrich the student's own grasp of the current educational scene.

3. **IMPROVEMENT OF TEACHING.** Every student of education who aspires to be an outstanding teacher can benefit by a knowledge of how educational practices developed.

4. **GREATER COMPREHENSION OF THE INTERRELATIONSHIP OF THE ELEMENTS OF EDUCATION.** Without some knowledge of educational history the student would be inclined to view education in individual segments of special methods, general methods, administration, principles of learning, curriculum and guidance. A course in educational history enables him to understand the development of each of these areas and to perceive how the elements are interrelated.

5. **IMPROVEMENT OF EDUCATION.** Since man must learn through experience, the study of the educational experiences of past ages and places may serve as a guide to improvement of the present.

6. **CULTURAL ENRICHMENT.** The student of educational history must read and study the great classics of our civilization. He assimilates in this manner an understanding of the basics of our culture.

7. **EDUCATIONAL EVALUATION.** The major reason for studying educational history is that a knowledge of history makes possible a sound evaluation of earlier educational institutions, theories and practices for the purpose of improving our present educational institutions, theories and practices. The problems, failures and successes of the past three millenniums of human effort to improve education have had their effect upon society and individuals. Knowledge of these factors can enlighten our educational future.

1 | ORIGINS OF EDUCATION

BEGINNINGS. Prehistoric men communicated with each other more by gesture than by sound. Spoken sounds, representing things and feelings, gradually developed into *primitive language* which could be understood even without gestures. This early language, containing *few abstractions*, served as a basis for the development of education. It helped primitive tribes to achieve two major *educational purposes:*

1. <u>DEVELOPMENT OF SKILLS.</u> Language helped elder tribesmen to teach the young one skills in hunting, animal husbandry, agriculture, and pottery.
2. <u>DEVELOPMENT OF ATTITUDES AND VALUES.</u> Language contributed to the development of attitudes and values designed to protect the individual and the tribe. Emphasis upon the importance of courage and bravery constituted the first effort at character education.

IMPACT OF WRITING. Written language has existed for about six thousand years. Written symbols were used to describe the *art of making pottery* and as a shorthand communication for *commercial purposes.* The early civilizations of the Middle East, an area stretching from Egypt to India, developed writing into a complex art. The priests and scribes of early Egypt and Sumeria were able to leave written records of the many achievements of their civilizations. Use of *the alphabet, paper, pen and ink* led to *the building of libraries* which stored up the treasured wisdom of the past.

THE EARLIEST SCHOOLS. The oldest known written records are of Sumerian origin, dating back to the middle of the fourth millennium B.C. *The schools* of the ancient civilization of Sumeria had the following characteristics:

1. <u>PRIEST TEACHERS.</u> Teachers were priests of the temple.
2. <u>TEMPLE AFFILIATION.</u> Schools were attached to the temples.
3. <u>COEDUCATION.</u> Boys and girls were educated together.
4. <u>CURRICULUM.</u> The curriculum included:

   a. <u>The Basics.</u> Reading, writing, and arithmetic were taught. Archeologists have recovered remains of school tablets containing pupil exercises in multiplication and division.
   b. <u>Patriotism.</u> The young were indoctrinated in patriotism. Teachers stressed loyalty to king and state, with emphasis on study of the lives of the kings and the history of wars and conquests.
   c. <u>Piety.</u> Religion was taught as a means of inculcating piety. Preservation of respect for the gods of Sumeria also meant perpetuation of the teacher-priests and temples.

INDIA

SOCIAL BASIS OF EDUCATION. The educational system of any society is both a product and a reflection of the culture in which it exists. To understand the causes and meaning of an educational system, therefore, it is necessary to examine the culture in which it is rooted.

THE ARYANS. The Aryans or "noble people" lived around the Caspian region in times before history was properly recorded. Under pressures of over-population and the need to trade, they *invaded the south*, conquering Sumeria in the west and the *primitive Nagas people of India* in the east. These white invaders, finding themselves a minority among the darker races in India, imposed strict regulations to protect their white identification. The "Varna" or color segregation rules formed the basis of the caste system and were incorporated into *the Hindu religion* of the conquerors.

THE CASTE SYSTEM. The Vedic social order was divided into the following four castes:

1. <u>BRAHMAN.</u> The highest caste, the Brahman, was comprised of those who were *responsible for the spiritual and educational direction* of society. The social and ritual duties of this caste were arduous. It also was the most protected caste in Hindu society. Death was the penalty for striking any Brahman.
2. <u>KSHATRIYA.</u> The ruling warrior caste, the Kshatriya, was responsible for *governmental administration*, war, politics, and public affairs.
3. <u>VAISHYA.</u> This caste was comprised of those who engaged in *trade and industry*, the merchant class.
4. <u>SHUDRA.</u> *Laborers* belonged to the caste called the Shudra. They were considered the *"untouchables" or outcasts* of society. Originally this caste was made up almost exclusively of the dark aboriginal people of India.

SOCIAL MOBILITY. In Hindu society there was no possible mobility from one caste to another. One was born into a caste and his *"dharma,"* or social rule, governed him for life. His only hope for upgrading his status lay in *reincarnation*. Suffering and punishment in a future life derived from one's failure to observe one's "dharma." An obedient life would bring the reincarnated soul into a higher caste. If a man were to marry outside his caste, his children would be treated as *pariahs* or untouchables. His wife could not assume the higher caste into which she married.

EDUCATION. Religion, philosophy, and individual experience in life were all one. *The Vedic scriptures of the Hindu religion governed every aspect of life.* Consequently, educational aims, the method of education, the teacher, and the pupil were governed by caste and "dharma," or rule of conduct. Moral training for obedience and self discipline began for all castes at age four. Formal Indian education for many centuries had the following characteristics:

1. DURATION OF EDUCATION.
   a. <u>The Brahman.</u> Since the Brahmin was responsible for counselling administrators and for upholding religion and knowledge, *his education had to be extensive as to time* as well as content. It was recommended that a Brahman study for thirty-six years. Although eighteen years of education was acceptable, in no case could a Brahman be educated for less than nine years. It was recognized that some Brahmans could learn at a faster pace than others.

b. **The Kshatriya.** Members of this caste, rulers or administrators, *shared the early nine-year training of the Brahmin. Three years of physical and military training* followed.

c. **The Vaishya.** Members of the merchant caste had the same basic nine-year education as those of the two higher castes. Then their education stopped. Because this caste was assumed to be less intelligent than higher castes, the formal education of its members began later than for their superiors, at about age eight.

d. **The Shudra.** No formal education.

2. **AIMS OF EDUCATION.** Academic training was less important in Indian education than *character training.* Learning the ritual governing one's caste, development of control over appetites of hunger and desire, and acquisition of attitudes of obedience, reverence, and acceptance of authority were of highest importance. These social values were taught to all three formally educated castes and were encouraged among the untouchables. Educational goals for each caste were:

a. **The Brahmin.** The Brahmin caste received, in addition to training for character, health, and etiquette, instruction in the Vedic scriptures, large sections of which had to be memorized. As a future dispenser of knowledge, the Brahmin child spent less time than other Indians in physical training and recreational games. He spent at least the first quarter of his life with one or more teachers for the purpose of *developing his spiritual knowledge and self control* to a point where, hopefully, he would be able to cope with any contingency in life.

b. **The Kshatriya.** The future military leaders of society were trained to *greater physical skill* than any other caste. The prime educational goal for them was to develop a capacity for political and military leadership.

c. **The Vaishya.** The aim of education for members of the merchant caste, considered less able intellectually, was to develop in them some *spiritual insight.* The economic training varied with each pupil and each teacher.

d. **The Shudra.** The untouchables, who received *no formal education,* were trained in whatever household or other laborious duties were to occupy them. Later, as adults, men and women listened to lectures given by the Brahmins. Any memorizing of the Vedic scriptures was forbidden the untouchables under pain of death.

3. **NO COEDUCATION.** Boys and girls were not educated together. Since after marriage a woman became her husband's property, her education was aimed only at developing *household competencies. The status of women was far below that of men,* although women of the Brahmin caste received limited instruction in the Veda.

4. **CURRICULUM.** Ancient Indian education stressed *theology, philosophy, religious ritual, ethics and vocational skills.* Later, grammar and philology were included in basic courses. There were stirrings of scientific thought in ancient India, but this area of learning was reserved for Brahmins exclusively. By the year 500 B.C., young Brahmins were receiving instruction in *mathematics, chemistry, physics, astronomy, and physiology.*

5. **TEACHING METHODS.** Two distinctly different methods of teaching were used for two classes of subjects in early Indian schools: religious subjects and all other subjects. Religious subjects, the Hindu scriptures in particular, were *taught by rote.* The student was required to memorize the acceptable answer to the teacher's question on the scriptures. The assumption was that the scriptures embodied ab-

solute truths which the student was not privileged to doubt. All other subjects were taught in such a manner as *to encourage classroom discussion and participation*. Individual *judgment* was considered more important to progress in learning than memory alone. *Corporal punishment* never was inflicted on the Brahmin student. For other castes this form of discipline was rare until after 500 B.C. when *use of the rod* to ensure good behavior became common.

6. **TEACHER-PUPIL RELATIONS.** The pupil was required to treat his teacher with *reverence and respect*. In dealing with Brahmin pupils, students of the lower castes were expected to act with humility, reverence, and friendliness. All pupils were required *to beg as mendicants for both their own and their teacher's food*.

7. **SCHOOL ADMINISTRATION.** Education was *free and universal* to all children not in the untouchable caste. The schools were *privately operated and privately supported by donations*.

INTENT OF INDIAN EDUCATION

1. **THE STATED AIM** of the system of education in India was identical with the aim of religion: *ultimate peace for the individual soul*. The members of each caste were provided with the moral discipline, knowledge, and skills necessary for them to work toward ultimate unity with the god Brahma in the blessed state of passionless bliss called nirvana. The concept of reincarnation permitted those of lower caste to hope for a future life on earth, in a different body, at a higher caste level, and to hope for a progression through further reincarnations to the achievement of nirvana.

2. **PRACTICALITY OF THE SYSTEM.** The educational system of India offered the pupil a pathway to tranquility and peace through the self-disciplined control of his lower appetites and desires. Practically, the system also worked to keep the members of each caste, in their present life, reconciled to doing the work decreed for them by the Brahmins without complaint.

CHINA

INTRODUCTION. In China, up to the present century, education and Confucius were, in the public mind, synonymous terms. If one was educated, one knew the works of Confucius. Yet it was almost three hundred years after the death of Confucius in 479 B.C. that schools reaching beyond a select few were started during the Han dynasty (206 B.C. to 221 A.D.). It was more than a thousand years after Confucius' death that educational practices which were to be followed for centuries were formalized in an attempt at more widespread education under the Tang dynasty (618 A.D. to 906 A.D.). *The philosophy and teachings of Confucius were the strongest influence* in early Chinese education. A secondary important influence was *Lao-tze*, who preceded Confucius in history and who was, according to his critics, a sponsor of "anti-educational thinking." Lao-tze nevertheless had followers who adopted his philosophy with religious fervor.

LAO-TZE. The name of this teacher-philosopher means simply "the old master." Little is known about the life of Lao-tze (probable dates: 604 to 531 B.C.) and his sole surviving work is the "Tao-Te-Ching" or "The Book of the Way and of Virtue." This work presents three aspects of his philosophy. The three are:

1. **TAOISM.** The key to wisdom is found in the *imitation of the ways of nature*. The good life is a simple rustic life of contemplation.

2. <u>**ANTI-INTELLECTUAL.**</u> *Knowledge is not virtue.* It is the source of the evils of ambition and contention. The worst possible government would be a government ruled by intellectuals. Man must imitate nature by his simplicity and silence. He can achieve tranquility through *the abandonment of knowledge*. He must suppress his thoughts and turn to a silent inward contemplation of nature.

3. <u>**IDEAL SOCIETY.**</u> Lao-tze believed that simple men living close to nature, with *the least possible number of laws and social regulations*, would be happy. Man ought to repudiate the city life in favor of the simple life in the country.

CONFUCIUS

IMPORTANCE. Confucius was *the most important influence* upon Chinese life and education. His teachings constituted the background of Chinese education for centuries, guiding its aims, content, and practice. The philosophy he propounded *has influenced Chinese society up to the present day.*

LIFE OF CONFUCIUS.

1. <u>**EARLY YEARS.**</u> K'ung Ch'iu or Kung-fu-tze (Confucius) *was born in the province of Shantung in 551 B.C.* His father died while he was a child. He began working to support his mother. *He married when he was nineteen years* old, had a son and two daughters. Four years later he divorced his wife.

2. <u>**TEACHER.**</u> In 529 B.C., at age twenty-two, *Confucius started a school* in one room of his house. Over the course of his lifetime he was to teach three thousand students. Of these students, Confucius regarded about eighty as outstanding.

3. <u>**CHIEF MAGISTRATE.**</u> Confucius earned public respect during thirty years of teaching and in 499 B.C. became the *chief magistrate* for the city of Chung-tu. His reforms made the city a model of governmental excellence.

4. <u>**VOLUNTARY EXILE.**</u> After six years as chief magistrate, Confucius had a disagreement with the ruler of the city who had ignored his counsel. He went into voluntary exile in 493 B.C.

5. <u>**RECALLED FROM EXILE.**</u> Ten years later, in 483 B.C., a new ruler recalled Confucius from exile following a military victory achieved by one of Confucius' students.

6. <u>**LAST YEARS.**</u> Confucius spent the remaining four years of his life in *teaching and writing.* These years were clouded by the tragic deaths of his only son and two of his favorite disciples. He died at age seventy-two in April, 479 B.C.

THE NINE CLASSICS. Confucius edited and occasionally wrote in the following *five canonical books:*

1. <u>**RECORD OF RITES**</u>
2. <u>**BOOK OF CHANGES**</u>
3. <u>**BOOK OF ODES**</u>
4. <u>**SPRING AND AUTUMN ANNALS**</u>
5. <u>**BOOK OF HISTORY**</u>

THE SHU BOOKS. The four books entitled Shu were *added by disciples* of Confucius. These four books together with the preceding five canonical books constitute the *Nine Classics* of China. *Students were required to learn whole sections of these classics by rote.* The final four books are:

1. <u>**DISCOURSES AND DIALOGUE**</u>
2. <u>**THE GREAT LEARNING**</u>
3. <u>**DOCTRINE OF THE MEAN**</u>
4. <u>**BOOK OF MENCIUS.**</u>

CONFUCIAN THOUGHT. Among *important theories and beliefs* propounded by Confucius are the following:

1. **AGNOSTICISM.** Confucius is *silent on metaphysical questions* as to the nature of God, Man and the Universe. A *harmony is sought between human conduct and nature*. The wise man is responsive to his duties toward his fellowman. He ought to respect the current religious beliefs but remain aloof from them.
2. **A DISCIPLINED SOCIETY.** The foundation of any good society is a well-disciplined individual in a disciplined family. The good order stemming from *obedience within the family* is the basis of social harmony.
3. **A DISCIPLINED INDIVIDUAL.** The aim of education is to develop a man who is both knowledgeable and of good character. The disciplined man has *three virtues: intelligence, courage, and benevolence.*
4. **THE IDEAL STATE.** The ideal *government realizes that it derives its authority from the people*. It continues in operation because the people give it respectful obedience. Aspects of good government are:

    a. **Good Example.** The state must be just and sincere. It sets an *example of good behavior* to all its members in this way.
    b. **Education.** The state must encourage public education. *Etiquette, history, and music ought to be studied by all*. However, a higher education ought to be given only to those who can profit from it.
    c. **Xenophobia.** *The fear of foreign nations and people* which characterized China's foreign relations for centuries originates from advice given by Confucius to avoid all foreign powers.
    d. **Rulers.** Men of *virtue and high ability* ought to be elected to government office.

5. **THE STATE OF SIMILARITY.** Confucius foresaw that day when the *entire world* would be *one single republic*. The government would consist of *elected men of virtue and intelligence*. This world republic would be a classless society where all men would treat all other men with the deference given to a parent. Such a utopia would find men working because they loathe idleness and sharing their wealth because they hate selfishness.

CHINESE EDUCATION. Education in China became widespread during the Tang dynasty (618 to 906 A.D.). It was encouraged by the state policy of conducting competitive examinations for appointment to public office.

CHARACTERISTICS OF CHINESE EDUCATION.

1. **PRIVATE TEACHING.** The school was located in *the home* of a teacher. The teacher charged a fee for each pupil.
2. **AIM.** The goal of education was the development of a *well-mannered man of character and judgment*.
3. **CURRICULUM.** The basic curriculum included reading, writing, etiquette, history and music. *The writings of Confucius* were the mainstay of reading courses. The student was required to memorize large sections of the *Nine Classics*. As the student advanced, he also studied *poetry and philosophy*.
4. **METHOD AND DISCIPLINE.** The usual teaching approach was catechetical. The teacher asked a question eliciting a specific response from the student. Discipline was maintained through physical punishment when necessary.

5. **TEACHER-STUDENT RELATIONSHIP.** The teacher expected to find an eager, motivated, hard-working student. The student began his daily lessons at eight o'clock in the morning and studied until five in the evening. During the summer the school day ended at noon, freeing the student for farm work in the afternoon.

6. **EXAMINATIONS FOR PUBLIC OFFICE.** Students who aspired to public office were required to pass *provincial examinations.* These examinations were conducted regularly in all provinces. Questions were based largely upon the *Nine Classics.* A student who passed his examination was considered to be a member of the literary class. Additional examinations were required for advancement in national office.

2 | EARLY EDUCATION IN EGYPT, PERSIA AND ISRAEL

EGYPT

EGYPTIAN CIVILIZATION. *The civilization of ancient Egypt was one of the oldest in the world.* It was highly developed by the fourth millennium B.C. and its sophistication and complexity increased down through some thirty centuries. Eventually this civilization influenced Persian, Greek, and Roman invaders and conquerors and, through them, our present civilization.

EGYPTIAN SOCIETY.

1. **ABSOLUTE MONARCHY.** From the earliest government of the "Old Kingdom," established in about 4,000 B.C., through the many dynasties of the "Middle Kingdom" and the "New Kingdom," *the Pharaoh ruled the Egyptian empire with absolute authority.*
2. **EXTENT OF EMPIRE.** The Egyptian empire varied from one epoch to another in the extent of its foreign possession but always, under the Pharaohs, it embraced numerous conquered territories and a variety of peoples beyond the boundaries of Egypt proper.
3. **DURATION OF EMPIRE.** The Egyptian empire *lasted longer than any other sovereign state up to the present time.* From its beginnings in the dim past of prehistory, Egypt remained autonomous until conquered by the Persians under Cambyses in 525 B.C. Later, in 332 B.C., it was captured by the Greeks under Alexander. In 30 B.C. it was reduced to the status of a province of the Roman empire. Thus ancient Egypt, from rise to fall, enjoyed an *unexampled duration of approximately 3,000 years.*
4. **THEOCRACY.** *The Pharaoh was considered to be divine,* the descendant of gods and a god himself. His absolute authority rested solidly upon the Egyptian religion and he in turn gave support and sanction to the priests who nurtured that religion.
5. **RELIGION.** The Egyptians were sun worshippers. The chief god among their many gods was *Amon, the Sun God,* also called, at different times and in different localities, Re. The priests were powerful in the government. They had wealth and prestige. They were responsible for the activities of the temples, they controlled both secular and religious education, they performed governmental functions and were influential advisors to the Pharaoh. The power of the priests helped religion to hold its place as a dominant force throughout the history of ancient Egypt. The masses of people accepted the official religion without question. They believed that piety in this life would be rewarded with eternal life after death.
6. **CLASS DIFFERENCES.** Egyptian society was divided into distinct classes:

   a. **The Aristocracy.** This class was made up of two groups: (1) administrators of noble family related by blood to the family of the Pharaoh and (2) the priests.
   b. **The Middle Class.** Merchants, skilled craftsmen and scribes belong to the middle class.

    c. <u>The Lower Class</u>. This class was made up of the large body of farmers and laborers who, though technically free, were poor.

    d. <u>The Slaves</u>. Slaves were the property of the wealthier classes.

7. <u>ECONOMY</u>. In the beginning, Egyptian economy depended upon agriculture. Later, *trade became an economic mainstay*. Land caravans enabled traders to reach Egypt's conquered provinces; ships took them to foreign ports along the Mediterranean Sea. Trade was a major factor in building up the enormous wealth of ancient Egypt.

8. <u>CULTURE</u>. Egypt produced *the world's first literature*. This achievement was made possible by the early development of *writing*; it was made easier by the early adoption of paper (papyrus) as a replacement for stone tablets. The vast mass of writing left by the ancient Egyptians includes business and legal documents; historical, educational, philosophic and scientific literature; instruction for artists and craftsmen; magical, astrological, and religious materials; and the first written works of *fiction and poetry*. The Egyptians were the world's first great builders. Their outstanding accomplishments in *architecture* required an impressive knowledge of *physics and mathematics*. The arts of *painting and sculpture,* first designed to provide ornamentation for the tombs of the dead, later served to enrich many areas of living. *Wood carvings* found on ornamental furniture indicate an artistic ability surpassing mere craftsmanship. Egyptian astrology was the forerunner of modern *astronomy*.

9. <u>INFLUENCE</u>. The achievements of Egypt during its long ages as an independent and wealthy center of culture and government made a strong impression upon the nation's conquerors. Large portions of Egyptian knowledge and skill in science, art, architecture, literature, government, and education *were assimilated by the Persians, the Greeks, and the Romans*. Egyptian knowledge was synonymous with wisdom in ancient Greece. The present-day civilizations of all western countries are *indebted to Egyptian culture*.

EDUCATION IN ANCIENT EGYPT

PURPOSE OF EDUCATION. The primary aim of Egyptian education was to prepare young men for careers as scribes, priests and government officials.

THE EDUCATIONAL SYSTEM. In general the child inherited the class and the occupation of his father. He received training in the skill of his father at home. *Formal education* was conducted under the guidance of the priests. There were two types of school:

1. <u>THE TEMPLE SCHOOL</u>. The early education of the child was conducted at the temple. The child studied reading and writing, and learned the religious legends of Egypt.

2. <u>THE STATE SCHOOL</u>. Schools of higher education, giving advanced instruction to prepare young Egyptians for service to the state, were organized and supported by the government and were staffed by priests as administrators and teachers. The curriculum stressed literature, mathematics, and the sciences.

DISCIPLINE. Punishment was used to compel learning. The slower learner was struck on the back with a stick.

METHOD. While learning by rote was one method of acquiring information, the Egyptians, more than any other ancient people, *relied upon the written page* as a tool of education.

PERSIA

BEGINNINGS. During the second millennium B.C., continuing waves of Aryan migrations, starting from the Aryan homeland north of the Caspian Sea, moved eastward to Italy and Greece, westward to India, and southward to the Middle East. The immigrants to the Middle East formed the population of what was to become the Persian empire.

PERSIAN SOCIETY.

1. <u>**ABSOLUTE MONARCHY.**</u> The Persians were ruled by *a king with absolute authority* derived from the gods.
2. <u>**SIZE AND DURATION OF THE EMPIRE.**</u> The Persian empire lasted from about 2000 B.C. until conquered by Alexander The Great in 330 B.C. This empire, centered in what is now Iran, included the entire Middle East from Egypt to the borders of India. After the failure of Darius to capture Greece, the empire began to decline. It was destroyed by Alexander after his conquest.
3. <u>**CASTE SYSTEM.**</u> The caste into which a man was born determined his position for life. Persia had three castes:
   a. <u>**The Noble.**</u> This caste owned land. It was composed of governmental rulers, military leaders and priests.
   b. <u>**The Farmer and Laborer.**</u> The workers of this caste were also the conscripts who served in the armies.
   c. <u>**The Slave.**</u>

4. <u>**RELIGION.**</u> The religion of ancient Persia is called *Zoroastrianism.* Its teachings closely parallel those of Christianity. The prophet Zoroaster is said to have lived about 1000 B.C. Legend claims he was born miraculously of a noble virgin. His life was spent teaching the doctrine that Ahura-Mahzda was the supreme *God of Light,* who would eventually triumph over the God of Darkness with whom he was in continual conflict. At death the soul would be rewarded for its virtue by eternal life with the God of Light. The wicked would be punished with eternal torment. At the final judgment the souls of the just would be returned to their bodies to live in perfect bliss.

EDUCATION IN ANCIENT PERSIA

PURPOSE OF EDUCATION. The major purpose of education in Persia was to develop a pious individual who was worthy of eternal life and a courageous able warrior capable of protecting the state.

THE EDUCATIONAL SYSTEM. A child born into either of the two lower castes received training at home in the skills of his father. *Formal education* existed only for the nobility. It was conducted under the guidance of the priests. Four classifications of education for the nobility were:

1. <u>**EARLY EDUCATION.**</u> Children remained with their mothers until age 5. From age 5 to 16 they received basic training designed to promote physical strength, good health habits, good character, and pious attitudes toward religion.
2. <u>**SECONDARY EDUCATION.**</u> From age 16 to 25 the pupil was instructed in *law, government administration, military tactics, rudimentary mathematics, and religion.*

3. **HIGHER EDUCATION OF THE PRIEST.** Students who wished to become priests were given further training in the *ritual and beliefs of Zoroastrianism.*
4. **MEDICINE.** Students at the secondary educational level could choose to become physicians. Those who made this choice received instruction in the *medical beliefs of the time.*

DISCIPLINE. Discipline was administered harshly by the stern and stoical priests. The object was to inculcate *strength of character* which would enable the pupil to hold fast to virtue and to endure whatever physical or mental hardships he might meet in his later life.

METHOD. *Textbooks were not used in ancient Persia.* The teacher told the pupils stories calculated to indoctrinate them in habits and attitudes favorable to piety and patriotism. Pupils were required to memorize and repeat these lessons by rote.

ISRAEL

IMPORTANCE. The culture of the ancient Hebrews is of great importance to contemporary western civilization. Hebrew thought regarding God and man became a major moving force of western civilization. The contemporary emphasis in American society upon *the dignity of the individual man and the importance of freedom* owes its origin to Hebrew thought.

HEBREW OR JEW. Although the two terms, Hebrew and Jew, now are used interchangeably, Hebrew is the older, generic, term. It was applied to all of the Semitic tribes living in Palestine from the time of the first settlement. The term Jew originally meant specifically "one belonging to the tribe of Judah or (see below) to the kingdom of Judea." After the return of the Hebrews from exile in Babylonia the term Jew came to mean any member of the new united Hebrew state, Israel. The ancient tribes of Palestine now are referred to as either Hebrew or Jewish. The people of Israel were and are also called Israelites.

ANCIENT HEBREW SOCIETY

HISTORICAL MILESTONES. Historical events and circumstances of importance to the development of the Hebrew nation were:

1. **BEGINNINGS.** The Hebrews were Semitic nomads who settled in Palestine during the second millennium B.C.
2. **DELIVERANCE FROM EGYPTIAN SLAVERY.** Hebrews enslaved in Egypt escaped under the leadership of Moses. After forty years they arrived in Palestine, defeated the native Canaanites, and regained possession of their former homeland.
3. **SAMUEL AND SAUL.** Samuel and Saul united the various Hebrew tribes into one political kingdom in order to meet the military threat of the Philistines.
4. **DAVID AND SOLOMON.** The final defeat of the Philistines was brought about under the leadership of King David. This made possible the golden age of the ancient Hebrew nation under David's son, Solomon.
5. **TWO KINGDOMS.** In 930 B.C. the ten northern tribes revolted from the government of the House of David. They set up a new kingdom called Israel, with Samaria as its capital. The kingdom of Judea retained Jerusalem as its capital.
6. **THE ASSYRIAN CONQUEST.** In 720 B.C. the Assyrians invaded Israel and destroyed

the kingdom. The ten tribes were taken into bondage.

7. **THE BABYLONIAN CONQUEST.** In 586 B.C. the Babylonians, having defeated the Assyrians in Israel, then destroyed Judea. The two tribes of Judea were taken into slavery.

8. **PERSIAN PROTECTORATE.** The Persians destroyed the Babylonian empire. In 536 B.C. Cyrus, the Persian king, returned the Hebrews in Babylonia to Jerusalem. At the time of the return, the Hebrews, regardless of which tribe they belonged to, began to refer to themselves as Jews, thus identifying themselves with the ancient kingdom of Judea and with its chief city, Jerusalem. The new political entity became a Persian protectorate and remained one until conquered by Alexander The Great. Later Syria, and, then Rome, conquered this territory.

9. **ROME.** The Emperor Titus put down a rebellion by destroying the city of Jerusalem in 70 A.D. The Jews remained without a country until 1948.

SOCIAL STRUCTURE.

1. **THEOCENTRIC.** The ancient Hebrew believed himself a member of *a race especially chosen by God.* God was the center of his social life and of his individual life. By following the law of the one God, Jehovah, he would, he believed, prosper. By deviating from that law, he would suffer.

2. **SOCIAL CATEGORIES.** *Social equality* existed among the Hebrews to an extent unusual for the time. The nation was organized into twelve tribes and every Hebrew belonged to one of the tribes. All tribes except that of Judah had equal standing in society. The tribe of Judah enjoyed some pre-eminence. In the early kingdom, Hebrew kings were of the tribe of Judah and it was believed that *the Messiah* would come from that tribe.

   a. **The Priests.** The Hebrew priesthood was *established by birth.* Only descendants of Aaron, the brother of Moses, and of the tribe of Levi, were eligible to become priests. The position of priest offered security but little opportunity to obtain great wealth. Priests were supported by the rest of the nation but they were not permitted to own land.

   b. **The Prophets.** Upon occasion, men of extraordinary virtue served as *guides, advisors, and stern preachers of* morality to king and people. It was believed that the prophets were divinely appointed and that they reflected the will of God.

   c. **The Kings.** The kings were subject to divine law and judgment just as the people were. The king's office was inherited, descending through the House of David.

   d. **The People.** The people were *equal to each other in both rights and obligations.* They were equal to the kings *in the eyes of God.* The people—and priests, prophets, and kings as well—were required to worship God and follow his commandments.

EARLY HEBREW EDUCATION.

1. **AIM.** The basic aim of Hebrew education was religious. It was necessary for all Hebrews *to know and follow the law of God.*

2. **FORMAL EDUCATION.** Before the Babylonian captivity, all education took place in the home. The father was responsible for the education of his son and the mother for that of her daughter. After the return from captivity, schools were organized to teach the growing amount of scriptural writings and interpretations. *The educational system* was divided into three parts:

a. **Ages Six Through Ten.** The child was taught to read and write. His religious instruction continued what he had learned in his home before the age of six. Teaching took place in the synagogue.

b. **Ages Six Through Sixteen.** Religious instruction continued with the rabbi as teacher. The pupil became acquainted with traditional writings and with the interpretation of Hebrew moral law.

c. **Higher Education.** Further study in moral and theological areas was carried on in an individual way under the guidance of learned men.

3. **EDUCATION FOR ALL.** All Hebrew children were educated equally. There could be *no educational privileges*, since all men were responsible for knowing and following the law.

4. **NATIONALISTIC.** The education of the individual served the God-centered nation. The basis of individuality was *the acceptance of God, His law, His people, and the divinely determined destiny of the Hebrew people.*

5. **EDUCATIONAL METHOD.** The teaching proceeded through *telling and repeating.* The content of learning was moralistic and students were expected to be able to apply the law of God to practical life situations.

3 | EARLY GREEK EDUCATION

IMPORTANCE. The value of early Greek education to western society cannot be over-emphasized. Many of *the current issues in our education* are similar to the issues that confronted education in ancient Greece. The achievements and the mistakes of the Greeks as they sought to improve education can serve as object lessons to help us solve our present educational problems. *Two conflicting views on education* existed side by side in two Greek city-states, Athens and Sparta. A flexible, *democratic view* prevailed in Athens, a rigid, *totalitarian view* in Sparta. The two cities, frequently at war on the battlefield, also were at war ideologically in the classroom. European heirs to Greek culture generally have favored the Athenian educational view over that of Sparta. *The goals, values, curriculum, and system of education* of ancient Athens continue to influence the present-day education of western countries.

HISTORICAL BACKGROUND. By the sixth century B.C., Greece was divided into *several hundred autonomous city-states*, each with its own government, laws, social institutions, and educational system. Although the city-states *united in the face of the Persian foe*, they returned to their separate entities following victory in the Persian wars. However, two city-states emerged as the unquestioned leaders of Greece — *Athens and Sparta.*

SPARTA

BACKGROUND. During the eighth century B.C. the Spartans conquered the southern Peloponnesus and enslaved the Helot inhabitants. Because they were surrounded by a hostile native population which outnumbered the conquerors, the Spartans established *a military state*. The rules controlling this government are attributed to Lycurgus, an early Spartan ruler.

SOCIAL ORGANIZATION.

1. <u>SUPREMACY OF THE STATE.</u> The Spartan citizen lived for the welfare of the state. From his birth until his death, the Spartan's life was regimented by the state. He possessed *no individual importance* apart from Sparta.
2. <u>COMMUNISM.</u> Each individual Spartan citizen was the property of the state. All members of the state *shared the land in common*.
3. <u>CLASSLESS.</u> Each male Spartan citizen belonged to *the Popular Assembly*. The Assembly elected *five Ephors* each year to rule the state. These Ephors had full political power.
4. <u>KINGS.</u> Two kings, sharing authority, *led the armies into battle*. The kingship was inherited. However, the office conferred *no special personal privileges*. In the early days of Spartan society, the kings had made the laws and had served as judges. After the Persian wars, these powers were taken from them and given to the Ephors.
5. <u>LIMITATIONS UPON FREEDOM.</u> Spartan citizens *could not leave the state* to

visit neighboring states. Foreigners were held in suspicion lest they corrupt the citizenry. The government *did not tolerate the arts, luxury, or intellectual pursuits.* The Spartan was trained toward self-discipline and sobriety.

6. <u>MILITARISM</u>. The *maintenance of military strength* was the most important aim and function of the Spartan government. Only invincible armies could guarantee the continued life of the city-state in the face of would-be conquerors.

7. <u>ECONOMY</u>. All *farming, trading, craftsmanship, and labor was done by slaves.* The Spartan citizen devoted his time to military and government affairs. All citizens dressed alike, regardless of position.

EDUCATION IN SPARTA

THE AIMS OF EDUCATION. Spartan education endeavored to develop character rather than mental acumen. The Spartan youth ideally would become an *obedient, disciplined, courageous and physically strong adult.* The ultimate objective of the educational system was to develop a loyal and patriotic warrior-servant of the state.

EDUCATIONAL SYSTEM.

1. <u>GIRLS</u>. Spartan women received *no formal education.* They were educated in the ideals of the state and in housewifery by their mothers at home. They were required to take gymnastics with other girls to increase their ability to bear strong and healthy children.

2. <u>BOYS</u>. Spartan boys were raised with strict severity by their parents until the age of six. *At six the Spartan boy was turned over to the state authorities.*

   a. <u>Barracks</u>. The Spartan boy after age six lived in a military barracks. He became a member of a unit of sixty-four boys of the same age. He was not permitted to live in a home again until he married at age thirty.

   b. <u>Paidonomous</u>. The Paidonomous was responsible for supervising the education of the youth. He was provided with assistants who conducted the training.

   c. <u>Cadet</u>. At age eighteen, the youth became a cadet to be trained for two years in military strategy and tactics.

   d. <u>Military Duty</u>. Between the ages of twenty and thirty, the Spartan young man was required to serve his country as a soldier at some military post.

   e. <u>Marriage</u>. At the age of thirty a Spartan man was required to marry. He then was given membership in the Assembly.

EDUCATIONAL CURRICULUM. The schooling of a Spartan youth consisted largely of *physical exercises, sports, military drill, and some discussion of feats of military heroism.*

DISCIPLINE. The discipline *was harsh* in the extreme. Flogging was the usual penalty for dereliction of duty. To encourage a capacity for physical endurance the youths were poorly fed and clothed. They walked without shoes and slept without blankets to inure them to cold and hardship.

ATHENS

BACKGROUND. In the fifth century B.C., Athens emerged from the Persian wars victorious, wealthy and cultured. During the period following the wars, called the age of Pericles, Athens was the *intellectual capital of the world.*

SOCIAL ORGANIZATION.

1. <u>DEMOCRACY.</u> Every free man had the right to vote and to participate in affairs of state. Each citizen was entitled to seek election as a leader. The democracy of Athens was *not a representative democracy*. Each citizen took *a direct hand* in the management of the state.
2. <u>ECCLESIA.</u> *An assembly of five hundred citizens* served as the law-making and judiciary body of Athens. Each citizen might serve no more than two terms in this body.
3. <u>CLASS STATUS.</u> All citizens possessed *equal rights*. The great wealth of some citizens gave them an unequal amount of comfort and luxury but it did not confer any added state privileges. *Women did not share the democratic rights* enjoyed by the men of Athens.
4. <u>SLAVERY.</u> The population of Periclean Athens contained seven slaves for every single free citizen. Most slaves were captured in warfare; some were obtained in trade from other city-states. *Slaves did all farming and other laborious work.* Crafts and skilled work were also assigned to slaves. Each citizen household had a number of domestic slaves.
5. <u>ECONOMY.</u> Athens became *the wealthiest city-state* following the Persian wars. Her imperialistic policies established *many colonies*, with which she traded. Through trade and conquest Athens grew rich.

EDUCATION IN ATHENS

AIMS OF EDUCATION. The purpose of education in Athens was to produce *a well-balanced individual*. Each citizen must be intelligent in order to fulfill the responsibilities of a free citizen, and of good character in order to serve and protect the state.

THE EDUCATIONAL SYSTEM.

1. <u>NO COMPULSORY EDUCATION.</u> Athenian citizens were not required to attend school. *Military training for two years* beginning at the age of eighteen was required of all without exception.
2. <u>EDUCATION FOR FREE MALE CITIZENS.</u> Only the sons of free citizens could receive an education. Girls were trained in household management by their mothers.
3. <u>ELEMENTARY EDUCATION.</u> From age seven to fourteen, the Athenian boy studied *reading, writing, music and gymnastics*. The school day began at dawn and ended at sunset. Schooling went on every single day of the year with the exception of religious festival days.
4. <u>INDIVIDUAL SCHOOLS.</u> Each school was *independent and privately operated* by a teacher. The state did not support education. The state did, however, supervise and regulate by law all elementary education.
5. <u>TEACHER STATUS.</u> The teacher of an elementary school occupied *one of the lowest* status positions in Athens. All of the teachers were men.
6. <u>SECONDARY EDUCATION.</u> Instruction beyond elementary levels was given by *itinerant teachers*. The curriculum depended largely upon the interests of the teacher. The subjects taught included *grammar, composition, speech, rhetoric, literature, music, mathematics, astronomy, and physics*. These schools were purely *voluntary* and were supported by *admission fees* paid by the pupils, whose ages ranged from fourteen to eighteen.
7. <u>MILITARY TRAINING.</u> *All male citizens* were required to enter military training

at age eighteen. During his first year the young recruit served within the confines of the city. In his second and final year he was placed on duty along the Athenian frontier. This training provided Athens with a skilled citizen army in times of war. Eventually military training in Athens gave way to higher education in philosophy, rhetoric, and science in one of the private academies.

SOCRATES

SIGNIFICANCE OF SOCRATES. Socrates developed a philosophy which, through his own teachings and the teachings of his immediate followers, especially Plato and Aristotle, eventually won the attention and respect of thinking men everywhere. The three great Socratic philosophers, Socrates, Plato, and Aristotle, were to be "rediscovered" during the Renaissance and their rational, practical, and scientific ideas were to *influence the thinking and the governmental, religious, and educational institutions of the entire western world.*

LIFE OF SOCRATES, 469-399 B.C.

1. <u>THE YOUNG SOCRATES.</u> Almost nothing is known of the childhood of Socrates but it can be assumed from his later display of learning that he attended the schools of Athens until he entered military service at age eighteen.

   a. <u>Military Hero.</u> Socrates served Athens in the warfare with Sparta, participating in the battles of Petidaea, Delium, and Amphipolis. In the course of the battle of Petidaea he saved the life of Alcibiades, the popular Athenian general.
   b. <u>Stonecutter.</u> Socrates worked from time to time as a stonecutter.
   c. <u>Sculptor.</u> He completed two works of sculpture, "Hermes," the god, and "The Three Graces."
   b. <u>Marriage.</u> Socrates married Xanthippe. She is said to have resented the fact that he charged no fees for his teaching. Later, in 415 B.C., Craco's Law authorized polygamy for the purpose of increasing the male population of the state. Socrates is believed to have taken a second wife at this time.

2. <u>PHILOSOPHER AND TEACHER.</u> Socrates devoted most of his adult life to the development of a philosophy and to teaching those followers who attached themselves to his dialogue discussion groups. Socrates was distinctive for:

   a. <u>Devotion to Ethics,</u> an attitude which influenced all later Greek philosophers.
   b. <u>Development of the Inductive Method</u> of reasoning.
   c. <u>Linking Knowledge to Happiness.</u> He believed that knowledge, or insight, was the foundation of virtue and happiness.
   d. <u>Rationalism.</u> Socrates believed that man was capable of arriving at truth through the use of reason.

3. <u>TRIAL AND DEATH.</u> Socrates, at age seventy, was brought to trial on charges that he was *an atheist* and *a corruptor of youth.* He was found guilty and was sentenced to death. On the order of his judges, Socrates drank poison hemlock and died. The trial and the last days and death of Socrates are described by Plato in the dialogues *Apology, Crito,* and *Phaedo.*

STUDENTS. Some of the famous men who studied with Socrates were:

1. <u>PLATO</u>, considered one of the greatest philosophers in the history of civilized man.
2. <u>ALCIBIADES</u>, a military genius.
3. <u>ARISTIPPUS</u>, founder of the Cyrenaic school of hedonism.
4. <u>ANTISTHENES</u>, founder of the Cynic school of philosophy.
5. <u>XENOPHON</u>, a military leader and historian.
6. <u>CRITO</u>, one of the wealthiest men in Athens.

SOCRATIC METHOD. Athens became the classroom of Socrates. He went about asking questions of authorities and of the man in the street in order to arrive at political and ethical truths. He questioned groups of his students as a means of instruction, to compel them to think a problem through to a logical conclusion. His *dialectic method,* or method of investigating problems through dialogue discussions, came to be known as the *Socratic method.* It involved:

1. <u>SOCRATIC IRONY.</u> Socrates pretended that he knew no answers. His assumed ignorance or willingness to learn from others was the background for adroit questioning to reveal the truth or expose the error of the answers he received.
2. <u>DEFINITION.</u> The initial question usually required the definition of the concept.
3. <u>ANALYSIS.</u> Subsequent questions elicited an analysis of the definition in all its implications.
4. <u>GENERALIZATIONS.</u> After examining all of the particular applications and consequences of the concept, Socrates reasoned, or persuaded his students to reason, from the particular to the general, or by the *process of induction*, to reach a general conclusion.

THE PHILOSOPHY OF SOCRATES. Although Socrates wrote no books, his philosophy is known through the writing of historians and of his students, and especially through the writings of Plato. Major ideas in the Socratic philosophy were:

1. <u>THE PROPER STUDY OF PHILOSOPHY IS MAN.</u> Socrates was not concerned with metaphysical questions as such. He believed that philosophy should achieve *practical results* in the form of greater well-being for man the individual and for mankind as a society. Hence, the proper study of philosophy is man. In pursuit of this study, Socrates' interests were centered in *ethics* and *politics*.
2. <u>NATURAL ETHIC.</u> Socrates attempted to establish an ethical system based upon human reason rather than upon theological directives.
3. <u>KNOWLEDGE AND WISDOM.</u> Socrates asserted that the highest good for any human being is *happiness.* Whatever action a man chooses is motivated by his desire for happiness. *Knowledge, virtue, and wisdom are all the same,* since man chooses an action according to what *he thinks* will bring him the greatest *happiness.* Therefore the more a man knows, the greater his ability to reason out the correct choice and to choose those actions which truly bring happiness to him.
4. <u>SELF-KNOWLEDGE.</u> The highest knowledge is possessed by that individual who truly knows himself. This knowledge constitutes ultimate wisdom. It enables man to act in a virtuous manner at all times, because he knows what will bring him true happiness.
5. <u>POLITICS.</u> Socrates did not approve of tyranny or of democracy. He believed that the best form of government was one ruled by an individual possessing the greatest ability, knowledge, and virtue.

THE EDUCATIONAL IMPLICATIONS OF SOCRATIC THOUGHT. The contributions of Socrates to education were:

1. **TEACHING METHOD.** The Socratic method offers the following advantages to the teaching act:

  a. **Problem Centered.** The dialectic begins with a problem which must be analyzed, e.g. "What is your opinion about the nature of justice?"

  b. **Based Upon Student Experience.** The student responds on the basis of his own knowledge and experience.

  c. **Critical Thinking.** The *student is held responsible* for his statements. The teacher analyzes some of the possible consequences of the student's remarks. The emphasis is upon the thinking processes of the student, who must think for himself and accept the consequences of his logic.

  d. **Teaching Is a Drawing Forth Rather Than a Telling.** In the Socratic method the teacher does not tell the student the proper answer. He draws from the student the probable answer.

  e. **Learning Is Discovery.** The student learns when he discovers the true generalization through his reasoning processes.

2. **PURPOSE OF EDUCATION DEFINED.** The aims of education as derived from Socratic thought are:

  a. **Self-knowledge.** The educated man is wise when he knows himself.

  b. **Individual Moral Good.** The acquisition of *knowledge* is valuable for man because it makes him *virtuous and happy*. Socrates repudiated any ornamental theory of knowledge. In similar fashion Socrates would deplore the use of knowledge merely for material success in life. Knowledge is ethically and morally important for all men.

  c. **Skill in Thinking.** Each man must develop his skill in critically appraising propositions through the reasoning process.

PLATO

LIFE OF PLATO, 427-347 B.C.

1. **FAMILY BACKGROUND.** Plato was born into an *aristocratic* and *wealthy* Athenian family. His *father* traced his ancestry in a direct line back to the *early kings* of Athens. His *mother* was the niece of the wealthy nobleman, *Critias* and the sister of the rich and famous *Charmides*. Both Critias and Charmides were students of Socrates.

2. **YOUTH.**

  a. **His Name.** Plato's given name was Aristocles, meaning "the best" and "renowned." He acquired the name of Plato in his youth because of his wide shoulders.

  b. **Outstanding Accomplishments.** He excelled in every area of youthful achievement. He was outstanding in sports, in music and in academics.

  c. **Military Hero.** During the war with Sparta, Plato won the Athenian prize for bravery.

  d. **Student of Socrates.** In 407 B.C., at the age of twenty, Plato became a student of Socrates.

4. **DISILLUSIONMENT WITH DEMOCRACY.** In 404 B.C. Plato witnessed the death of his uncle, Critias, during the civil war between the aristocrats and the democrats. Again, in 399 B.C., he witnessed the condemnation and execution of his beloved Socrates by the democratic regime led by Anyutus.

5. **VOLUNTARY EXILE.** Plato left his native city immediately following the execution of Socrates. He visited *Megara, Cyrene and Egypt.* After a brief return to Athens in 395 B.C., Plato continued his wanderings. In *Syracuse* he was sold into *slavery.* Plato raised three thousand drachmas through his friends to buy back his freedom. He returned to Athens in *387 B.C.*

6. **THE ACADEMY.** In 386 B.C. Plato purchased a recreation grove dedicated to the god Academus. This became the location of his school.

   a. **Tuition Free.** The students of the Academy paid no set fee. It was expected that the wealthier students would give gifts. It is believed that Dionysius II gave as his gift a sum equivalent to about a half-million dollars in American currency.

   b. **Coeducational.** Both men and women were welcome to study at the Academy.

   c. **Entrance Requirements.** The Academy accepted only advanced students who possessed a knowledge of *geometry.*

   d. **Curriculum.** The course of study included the following subjects:

      (1) **Higher Mathematics**
      (2) **Astronomy**
      (3) **Music**
      (4) **Literature**
      (5) **Law**
      (6) **History**
      (7) **Philosophy.**

   e. **Teaching Method.** Plato *lectured,* utilizing his vast knowledge to present an organized body of information to his students. He also made use of Socratic discussion by dialogue as a method of scientific investigation and instruction. At times problems would be assigned on an individual basis.

7. **LAST YEARS.** Plato *died around the year 347 B.C.* He continued to teach until the end, winning the admiration and love of his students and fellow Athenians.

8. **IMPORTANCE.** Plato is considered to be one of the most important philosophers of all time. His educational and philosophical theories continue to influence countless thousands. Whitehead, commenting on Plato's contribution to philosophy, said that every philosophy after Plato is but a footnote to Platonic thought.

THE PHILOSOPHY OF PLATO

PHILOSOPHY. These are some important aspects of Platonic philosophy:

1. **METAPHYSICS.** Ultimate reality is spiritual in nature. Plato explains in the *Timaeus* the necessity of postulating a prior *idea* or *form* for every material object. For example, the idea of a house must exist before the material shape can take place. Where any house exists, it conforms to the general idea of house.

   a. **The Nature and Destiny of Man.** Man has an individual soul chained to a material body. The soul is liberated at death. In *the tenth book of The Republic,* Plato states that the proper purpose of the soul is justice. The just soul will be rewarded by God following death. Suffering in life is the result of the evil one did in a prior existence. After man's death, the soul chooses its future body and destiny. "The gods are blameless."

2. **EPISTEMOLOGY.** Platonic epistemology was affected by consideration of:

   a. **Source of Knowledge.** Knowledge is a matter of recalling ideas that are innate in the soul.
   b. **A Priori Truths.** *All ideas are eternal and true.* Man does not know truth through the senses. The senses mislead and deceive man. Ideas are within man's soul. Man need not experience any outward events in order to know. He turns inward, making his life more spiritual and God-like, so that, free of the limitations of the senses, he approaches *the spiritual source of knowledge.*
   c. **Rationalism.** Each man is able to arrive at innate truths through *the use of his reason.*
   d. **Absolute Truth.** *All truths are eternal and absolute.* What is true today will always be true.
   e. **Test of Truth.** Something is known as true when the proposition in the mind is *logically consistent* with the eternal idea.

3. **POLITICS AND ETHICS.** Plato believed that justice is the most important virtue. Justice can exist only in a *just state.* Features of Plato's ideal state are:

   a. **Rule by the Best.** The ideal government would be ruled by the men or women *who demonstrate ability and aptitude* for ruling.
   b. **Organization of The Just State — Plato's Utopia.**

      (1) **The Guardians.** The ruling group would be made up of *philosopher-kings* especially trained for government administration. This group would never marry nor own property.
      (2) **The Warriors.** A group of warriors would be trained from youth in military skills in order to protect the state.
      (3) **The Workers.** This group would do all farming and other work necessary to feed the people.

   c. **Virtue.** The proper virtues for each group would include:

      (1) **Wisdom.** The ruling guardians would have wisdom.
      (2) **Courage.** The warriors would have courage.
      (3) **Temperance.** The workers would have temperance.

   d. **The Virtuous State.** The state would be just when its citizens had wisdom, courage, and temperance. Each citizen would serve the state to the best of his ability. Man would be an organism in the body of the state. The individual would be subordinated to the state.
   e. **Eugenics.** Although Plato would permit friendship between the sexes in his utopia, *the procreation of children would be controlled* by the government. Through the careful selection of mates, the race would be strengthened by improved children. Only men above the age of thirty and below forty-five, and women above the age of twenty and below forty, would be permitted to have

children. Any child born in violation of the state laws would be abandoned outside the walls of the city.

THE EDUCATIONAL THEORY OF PLATO

EDUCATION. Major ideas in Platonic educational theory are:

1. <u>**EDUCATION FOR ALL.**</u> Plato would educate every boy and girl to the limits of their abilities.
2. <u>**STATE EDUCATION.**</u> All children would *be taken from the parents* and educated by the state.
3. <u>**AIM OF EDUCATION.**</u>

     a. <u>Civil Servants.</u> To produce future servants of the state.
     b. <u>Rulers.</u> To develop virtuous intellectuals among the future rulers.
     c. <u>Warriors.</u> To glorify courage and military skill among the warriors.
     d. <u>Workers.</u> To develop competent, obedient, and temperate workers.
     e. <u>Social Disposition.</u> To develop a social disposition among all citizens.
     f. <u>Discipline.</u> To train the character of each citizen so that he may control his appetites, subordinating the senses to reason.

4. <u>**ORGANIZATION AND CURRICULUM.**</u>

     a. <u>Elementary.</u> All boys and girls would be educated together. They would study *mathematics, literature, poetry, and music* until they were eighteen years of age.
     b. <u>Military Training.</u> The next two years of the youth's life would be devoted to physical education alone. Thereafter, the best youths would be selected for the higher education given to future guardians of the state.
     c. <u>Higher Education.</u> Between the ages of twenty and thirty-five, the future guardian would receive a higher education to prepare him for ruling the state. His studies would include *mathematics, music, and literature.* At the age of *thirty* he would have enough maturity to begin his study of *philosophy.* At thirty-five, his formal education would cease and he would enter upon a minor administrative position, prior to undertaking more important governing positions.

5. <u>**TEACHING METHOD.**</u> Plato recommended making learning as close to *play* as possible on the elementary levels. Upon the higher levels of education, the student's reason would be trained in the processes of thinking and abstracting.

ARISTOTLE

LIFE OF ARISTOTLE, 384-323 B.C.

1. <u>**FAMILY BACKGROUND.**</u> Artistotle, born in *Stagire, Macedonia, in 384 B.C.*, was the son of a physician at the court of Amyntas, king of Macedon.
2. <u>**YOUTH.**</u> There are conflicting accounts of his early life. It is generally believed that Artistotle came to *Athens in 366 B.C.*, when he was eighteen years old, and became a *student in Plato's Academy.* Plato regarded Aristotle as brilliant and referred to him as the "nous" or "the mind."
3. <u>**MARRIAGE.**</u> About the year 344 B.C. Aristotle married Pythias, the sister of Hermias,

a student and friend of his. Hermias later became dictator of the city of Atarneus.

4. **TUTOR.** King Philip of Macedon appointed Aristotle, then age forty-one, as *official tutor of his son Alexander.* (This son later conquered the Persian empire and became known as Alexander the Great.) Aristotle succeeded Lysimachus who had taught the boy the basics of reading, writing, and arithmetic. Philip hoped Aristotle would help his son to avoid some of the evil excesses of life through the study of philosophy.

5. **UNIFICATION OF GREECE.** In 338 B.C. Philip of Macedon defeated the Athenian army at the battle of *Chaeronea.* He thereby effected the unification of Greece under Macedonian rule.

6. **THE LYCEUM.** Aristotle, now age fifty, moved to Athens once again. He purchased a valuable group of buildings, land and gardens, and there established a school of higher education in philosophy. The property had been dedicated to Appollo Lyceus and the school took its name, the Lyceum, from that of the god. Aristotle's Lyceum won acclaim for its distinguished work in the natural sciences.

7. **GROWTH OF SCIENCE.** When Alexander returned from his expeditions of conquest, he brought back to his former tutor Aristotle samples of animal and vegetable life from all over the conquered territories. Alexander also endowed Aristotle's school with the equivalent of almost four million dollars. Thus Aristotle was able to establish the first zoo and the first botanical garden in the world. Aristotle's scientific observations became the world's chief source of scientific knowledge for the next thousand years.

8. **TEACHING.** Aristotle continued teaching in the Lyceum until 323 B.C. In the morning, he strolled about the gardens with his regular students. The Greek descriptive word for "walking about" came to be applied to the school itself. Thus the school was *"peripatetic,"* and its students and adherents were "peripatetics." Aristotle always took his noon meal with his regular students. In the afternoon, he delivered lectures on politics, literature, and philosophy to the populace in general.

   a. **The Lyceum.** Two distinctive features among many at the Lyceum were:

   (1) **Student Rule.** *Students at the Lyceum organized and ruled themselves. Every ten days* a different student would be *elected to handle the administrative duties.*

   (2) **Student Research.** All students were assigned tasks involving *historical or scientific research.* Aristotle based many of his scientific propositions upon this research.

9. **LAST YEARS.** Aristotle had publicly supported Macedonian policies which were hateful to the subjugated Athenians. But he found continued support increasingly difficult as Alexander, flushed with conquest, became more arrogant and more capricious in cruelty. The political climate of Athens became dangerous for everyone, and especially for an independent philosopher. Aristotle broke with Alexander after he, Alexander, had Callisthenes, nephew of Aristotle, put to death for failing to reverence the ruler as a god. Aristotle went into exile, moving to Chalcis in Euboea in 323 B.C. He died this same year in Chalcis at age sixty-one.

THE PHILOSOPHY OF ARISTOTLE

PHILOSOPHY. A full presentation of the philosophical thought of Aristotle would require many volumes. However, some of the important points of that thought which influence the *Aristotelian educational theory* can be summarized briefly. Those points are:

1. <u>METAPHYSICS.</u>

    a. <u>Reality.</u> The universe is composed of two ultimate entities, *spirit or form and materiality or matter*. All things are reducible to one or other of these basic entities.

    b. <u>The Nature of Man.</u> Man is *a rational animal*. He is animal in his possession of a body with its physical needs and appetites. He is rational because he has a soul. The *active element of the soul* is part of the universal principle of life. This element is immortal. The *passive element of the soul* is the individual *personality*, with memories and thoughts relating to the experiences of life. This passive element ceases to exist with death. The soul and body form a necessary whole for the existence of the organism. The implications of this theory are:

       (1) <u>Destiny.</u> Man has no eternal destiny. *He ceases to exist as an individual personality at death.*

       (2) <u>Nature.</u> The *highest faculty in man is his spiritual nature*. Man acts according to his nature when he subordinates his physical appetites to reason.

    c. <u>Teleology.</u> There is purpose, order and intelligence in the universe, stemming from the first being, the unmoved Mover, God.

2. <u>EPISTEMOLOGY.</u>

    a. <u>Source of Truth.</u> The *faculty of reason* in every man can be trained, through the principles of logic, to reason toward true conclusions.

    b. <u>Nature of Truth.</u> *Truth is objective.* For example, a true proposition does not depend upon the mind of the individual man for its existence. Truths exist in nature and are discoverable by the reason of man.

3. <u>ETHICS.</u>

    a. <u>Happiness.</u> *The highest good* to which man may aspire is happiness. A truly happy life can be assessed only upon its completion.

    b. <u>Naturalism.</u> A man lives happily when his actions are in accordance with his nature. *Man's spiritual nature is superior to his physical nature.* The highest good for any man is the activity of his soul.

    c. <u>Reason.</u> The faculty of reason, resident in the soul of man, must *guide his every action*. The physical appetites must be controlled by reason. Reason, therefore, is the source of virtue.

    d. <u>Virtue.</u> Man uses his reason to judge between the extremes of any given act. *The middle course constitutes virtue.* For example, the mean between the two extremes of the vice of rashness (excess of courage) and the vice of cowardice (lack of courage) is the virtue of temperate courage.

4. <u>POLITICS.</u>

    a. <u>Purpose.</u> The purpose of the state is to produce human good.

    b. <u>Naturalism.</u> Man is social by nature. He will naturally be political. The difficulty in political philosophy is to *determine* how man may *act reasonably and virtuously to achieve the best political action.*

    c. <u>Reason.</u> The ideal state must be reasoned as a mean between two governmental extremes.

    d. <u>Constitutional Monarchy.</u> The best form of government is a constitutional monarchy, which is the mean between the extremes of despotism and democracy. The constitution guarantees moderation between the demands of the wealthy and the interests of the poor.

    e. <u>Public Education.</u> *The state is perpetuated through the education of its citizens.* Therefore education is, of necessity, *public in nature.*

THE EDUCATIONAL THEORY OF ARISTOTLE

EDUCATION. The importance of education in the philosophy of Aristotle was great, since the individual man could learn to use his reason to arrive at virtue, happiness, and political harmony only through the process of education.

1. <u>**AIM OF EDUCATION.**</u> The purpose of education is *to produce a good man.* Man is not good by nature. He must learn to control his animal activities through the use of reason. Only when man behaves by habit and reason, according to his nature as a rational being, is he capable of happiness. Education must aim at *the development of the full potentialities* of each man. It must seek the development of man's intellectual capacities to their fullest extent. It must aim also at developing each individual's body to its highest level of health and strength.

2. <u>**EDUCATION OF WOMEN.**</u> Women were considered *inferior to men.* The nature of women suggested that their proper function was fulfilled exclusively in the home. Women would not be educated with men. They would receive training in *gymnastics and domestic arts* to enable them to manage households, to bear and raise children, and to please and be obedient to their husbands.

3. <u>**EDUCATION OF MEN.**</u> Since citizenship would extend only to the aristocracy, which included rulers, soldiers, and priests, education would be given exclusively to this group. The farmer, laborer, merchant, and slave would be trained in whatever specific skills were required of them. Training in industrial arts or vocational skills is not education. Education is that which *liberates man,* enabling him to live his leisured existence according to his full potentialities. Education is therefore a practical means to the end of achieving the acme of man's nature.

4. <u>**THE CONTENT OF EDUCATION.**</u> Education *must not serve* any mean or vocational activity. These activities are the functions of slaves. The subject material must train the future rulers in the use of reason. Future rulers must learn obedience and responsibility before they rule. We may infer from *the curriculum of the Academy* that the following subjects would be taught:

    a. <u>Basics.</u> These would include *reading, writing and mathematics* (not for purposes of trade, but as a preparation for the intellectual abstractions of higher mathematics).

    b. <u>Natural Sciences.</u> Aristotle *emphasized* the natural sciences of astronomy, biology, physiology, zoology, chemistry and physics.

    c. <u>Physical Education.</u> The training of the body is important to the physical well-being of every citizen.

    d. Humanities. *Rhetoric, grammar, poetry, politics and philosophy* would be important subjects. During the early education of the child, Aristotle would have the state legislature censor the material which would be read by children.

5. <u>**THE METHOD OF EDUCATION**</u>. Aristotle placed *habit* high in the learning process. *Man learns by nature, by habit, and by reason.* Consequently, the teacher would organize materials according to the laws of reason. Repetitive drill would be used to reinforce what was understood by reason.

4 | ROMAN EDUCATION

BACKGROUND. Historical and social facts provide us with a background to understand the purposes, methods, organization and theory of *education in ancient Rome*.

1. <u>ROME AS CITY-STATE</u>. The *Latins* were Indo-European people who founded the city of Rome about 1000 B.C. The *Etruscans*, migrants from Asia Minor, ruled Rome from 655 B.C. to 508 B.C. The Etruscan king was called the Tarquin. During most of this period, the free citizens had a vote in governmental affairs but toward the end of it the power of the Tarquin became absolute. The two voting classes of society during this period were:

   a. <u>Patricians.</u> The upper-class Romans who ruled the important clans of the city were called Patricians. These leaders were *members of the Roman Senate.*
   b. <u>Plebeians.</u> The plebeian class was made up of all the remaining free citizens of Rome. These laborers, farmers, craftsmen and merchants *were members of the Assembly,* which voted upon questions of government, but had little power. It was dominated by the Senate.

2. <u>ROME AS A REPUBLIC</u>. The last Tarquin, Superbus, ruled with such cruelty that the Patricians deposed him and set up an *oligarchic republic*. The make-up of the Senate and the Assembly remained unchanged, but executive power was vested in elected officials.

   a. <u>Two Consuls.</u> Two patricians were elected as consuls to head the government. Their term of office was short: one year. Some consular responsibilities were delegated to:

      (1) <u>Praetors.</u> The Praetors were Roman military leaders and provincial governors.
      (2) <u>Censors.</u> Public servants, called Censors, determined the competence of minor officials and classified those eligible for military service.

3. <u>ROME AS A NATION</u>. Between 508 and 272 B.C., the Republic of Rome *systematically assimilated* all the people on the Italian peninsula.
4. <u>ROME AS AN EMPIRE</u>. The Roman republic emerged victorious over the empire of Carthage in a series of *three Punic Wars* that lasted from 264 B.C. to 146 B.C. The city of Carthage, in North Africa, was destroyed by *Scipio*. Between 201 and 146 B.C., Macedonia and Greece fell to Rome. A series of wars in the first century B.C. extended Roman power over the entire Middle East. With the conquest of Egypt by Caesar, *Rome ruled from England to the borders of India*. The struggle among Roman leaders for personal power over this vast empire ended when Octavian defeated Antony at Actium. *Octavian was proclaimed the Emperor Augustus in 27 B.C.*, with all legislative, judicial and executive authority vested in his person. This ended the Roman republic.

SOCIETY DURING THE ROMAN REPUBLIC

THE REPUBLIC. During the existence of the republic, from 507 to 27 B.C., outstanding features of Roman society were:

1. **PATRIARCHAL POWER.** The father of each family was the *undisputed head of the family*. His wife held a higher place in family life than wives of the Grecian civilization. Yet the father *held power of life and death* over his children.
2. **PATRONAGE.** Roman society was marked by its system of patronage, which grew until everyone was affected by it toward the end of the Republic. *Each man had a patron* to whom he could turn for aid and financial assistance. In turn the patron might expect praise and public adulation from his subordinates.
3. **AUTHORITARIANISM.** The most important virtue in Roman society was *strict obedience and respect for authority*. Uncritical acceptance of authority was a factor in the Roman military success.
4. **SLAVERY.** Every free Roman family had at least one slave in its household.

THE CONQUEST OF GREECE. Shortly before the Punic Wars, the Roman legions seized the Greek colonies in southern Italy. During the second century B.C., Rome conquered Macedonia and subsequently Greece. This acquisition of territory was of great significance for the following reasons:

1. **SLAVES.** It brought thousands of Greek slaves into Roman households.
2. **CULTURE.** Rome became familiar with the great cultural contributions of Greece to civilization.
3. **EDUCATION.** Often the Greek slaves were more educated than their Roman masters. These slaves became valuable as educators of Roman youth. *The educational theories of Greece were adopted by the Romans.*
4. **PHILOSOPHY.** The *Stoic* philosophy of the early Republic found its voice in the *Greek slave, Epictetus*. The basic ideas of *Stoicism* were:

    a. **Fate.** The life of every man is pre-determined in every detail. Since man can do nothing to alter his destiny, he achieves a good and happy life by mastering his desires and doing his duty.
    b. **Tranquility.** The man who is the master of his desires to the point where he is concerned only with those things within his power of possession, can arrive at a state of tranquility. This tranquility is achieved by:

        (1) **Control.** Man must control his desires.
        (2) **Duty.** He must carry out his duties.
        (3) **Reality.** He must *think realistically* of himself and the world.

THE IMPORTANCE OF STOICISM. The philosophy of Stoicism *gave stability to the government*. The ideals of strict obedience, resignation to one's lot in life, and performance of one's duty without question, helped to provide the state with good soldiers and obedient citizens.

THE PHILOSOPHY OF EPICURUS. Epicurean philosophy became a dominant influence among the upper classes and the wealthier Romans. In the later days of the republic, the large majority of the free Roman population, the Plebeians, lived upon doles or handouts from the government and individual patrons. The minority population of aristocratic Patricians and Equestrians (wealthy business men and bankers) lived lives of unparalleled luxury. It is understandable that Epicurean thought found ready acceptance among these privileged Romans. Here is a summary of major thoughts in the philosophy of Epicurus:

1. <u>PLEASURE.</u> The criterion by which one evaluates all human acts is the principle of pleasure. Whatever is pleasurable is good and whatever is painful is evil.
2. <u>HIERARCHY OF PLEASURE.</u> Pleasures are never bad. Some pleasures, however, are more necessary than other pleasures. Necessary pleasures are related to the needs of human existence.
3. <u>DESIRES NECESSARY FOR HUMAN EXISTENCE.</u> There are three human desires which provide necessary pleasure to man. These are desires for:

   a. <u>Ataraxia or Peace of Mind.</u> This is a state of inner tranquility which is achieved through *a life of moderate pleasure,* free of mental and physical pain.
   b. <u>Physical Health.</u> One cannot live without good health. *When the body is free of pain,* it is possible to enjoy pleasure.
   c. <u>Needs of Life.</u> All men require the security of food, shelter and clothing, before they can enjoy life. The *necessities of life,* along with *physical health and tranquility,* are desired as prerequisites for human well-being. Whatever pleasures interfere with any of these prerequisites are to be avoided.

4. <u>THE VIRTUE OF PRUDENCE.</u> The most important virtue is prudence. It is important because:

   a. <u>Evaluation.</u> Prudence enables one to evaluate the costs of various pleasures. It is sometimes necessary to suffer for a brief moment in order to achieve an enduring pleasure.
   b. <u>Self-control.</u> Man must not become a creature of impulse lest he sacrifice his peace of mind. It is necessary for him to practice a prudent control over his appetites.
   c. <u>Obedience to Law.</u> The prudent man obeys the laws. Laws are just in that they work toward the individual's security in the long run. Disobedience to the law results in pain or mental disturbance.
   d. <u>Retirement.</u> Through prudence, a man realizes that his well-being is best served by living a quiet life away from public turmoil. The imprudent man seeks public life, office and rewards, without counting the heavy cost to his tranquility.

5. <u>THE DESTINY OF MAN.</u> Each man must realize the limitations of human existence and live to the best of his ability a life of pleasure. There is *no reason to believe in the myths of religion. This life is all there is for him.* It is vital that he make it as pleasant as possible.

EDUCATION IN THE ROMAN REPUBLIC

THE OLD REPUBLIC. From 508 B.C. to 146 B.C., education took place in the home.

1. <u>RELATIVE TUTOR.</u> Young children were educated either by the mother or by an older family relative.
2. <u>CHARACTER TRAINING.</u> The child was trained to *strictest obedience.* He was taught early his place and duty in family and state.
3. <u>READING, WRITING AND ARITHMETIC.</u> The majority of Roman children acquired

an elementary knowledge of reading and writing. Arithmetic was never developed to a sophisticated extent because of the awkward method of writing numerals.

4. **APPRENTICE.** A young boy would learn his trade, skill or profession from his father or some male relative or friend of the family. Boys from upper-class families would actually follow their patron into the Senate in order to observe and learn how one argued a case.

EDUCATION AFTER THE CONQUEST OF GREECE

INTRODUCTION. Education in the Roman empire gradually absorbed the Greek educational ideal. By the first century B.C., influence predominated. Although the various schools sprung up without formal governmental regulation, the state came to regulate schools during the Principate of the Roman emperors. This formal school system, which influenced Europe until modern times, assumed the following forms:

1. **THE LUDUS.** At about *age seven*, the Latin child entered the Ludus or elementary school. He remained here until he was *twelve years old*. The *Magister*, or teacher, taught the children *reading, writing and arithmetic*. Discipline was harsh. The teacher struck disobedient children on the hand with a ruler or on the back with a leather strap. The pupil wrote with a stylus on a wax tablet. *Teaching was by rote*, and the child depended upon his *memory* to learn. Elementary schools were open to the children of all free families. *Children of upper-class families* learned elementary subjects from *private tutors*. *Many girls* attended the Ludus, but their education ended at this level.

2. **THE GRAMMAR SCHOOL.** The majority of boys entered grammar school at *age twelve* and remained until age *sixteen*. Both Latin and Greek grammar schools were available. Often youngsters would attend both types of school. Some characteristics of the grammar schools were:

   a. **Secondary Education.** These schools were the equivalent of contemporary secondary schools. Children from poor families rarely attended them.

   b. **Curriculum.** The teacher, called a grammarian, taught *grammar and literature*. The works of Homer and Virgil, with emphasis upon the Odyssey and the Aeneid, comprised the reading material.

   c. **Method and Discipline.** The teacher usually *lectured* to his classes. Students were expected to *take notes* and *memorize* these lectures. The *harsh discipline* of the Ludus continued through secondary school.

3. **THE SCHOOL OF RHETORIC.** Boys attended the school of rhetoric, the equivalent of our contemporary college, from age *sixteen* to *twenty*. Teachers were rhetoricians. They instructed students in grammar, argument, and speech.

4. **THE UNIVERSITY.** In the early years of the empire, two universities were established. The University of Athens and the University of Rhodes were well attended by adults. The age range of students was from *twenty-one* to *forty-five*. *Philosophy* was the principal subject. Other subjects covered were *law, mathematics, medicine, architecture, and rhetoric.*

QUINTILIAN

LIFE OF QUINTILIAN, 35-96 A.D. (?)

1. **EARLY YEARS.** Marcus Fabius Quintilian, *born at Calagurris*, Spain, about the year 35 A.D., was a member of a noble *patrician family*. He studied rhetoric in Rome

and returned to Spain. He married and had two children.

2. **SERVIUS SULPICIUS GALBA.** It is believed that Quintilian served as a lawyer for Galba, the governor of Spain from 58 to 68 A.D. After Nero was assassinated, Galba received word that the Praeterians had declared him Emperor. *Galba left for Rome, taking Quintilian with him.*

3. **TEACHER.** The Emperor Galba appointed Quintilian to head the most famous *school of rhetoric* in Rome. Although Galba fell into disfavor and ruled for only one year, Quintilian remained in Rome. His work in education won acclaim. Even the highly critical satirists *Juvenal and Martial* wrote with *great praise* of Quintilian.

4. **CHARACTER OF QUINTILIAN.** The writings of Quintilian and the judgment of his contemporaries reveal him to be a man of great intelligence, integrity, moral strength, and keen practicality. His love for his country and the students he taught was intense.

5. **TEACHING SUCCESS.** *Emperor Vespasian* appointed Quintilian to the *first state professorship of rhetoric* in Rome and he became one of the foremost teachers of his time. He retired in 88 A.D. to write. His famous *"Institutio Oratoria"* was begun at this time. *Emperor Domitian recalled him from retirement to* teach his two grandnephews. Quintilian is believed to have died about the year 96 A.D.

THE EDUCATIONAL THEORY OF QUINTILIAN

WORKS. The works of Quintillian are:

1. **"INSTITUTIO ORATORIA."** The "Education of the Orator" contains *twelve books*. Topics treated include:

   a. **Preschool Instruction.** Instruction in the home prior to schooling.
   b. **Curriculum.** The curriculum of the grammar school.
   c. **Rules.** The rules of public speaking.
   d. **Methods.** The methods of teaching.
   e. **Relations.** The relationship between student and teacher.
   f. **Lessons.** Sample lessons.
   g. **Style.** Advice on style in writing and speaking.
   h. **Practice.** Advice to the practicing orator.
   i. **Value.** The value of philosophy and law.

2. **"DECLAMATIONES."** This work is a collection of Quintilian's classroom exhortations, some of which were taken from the notes of Quintilian's students.

OBJECTIVES OF EDUCATION. Quintilian viewed education in practical terms. Its immediate purpose was to train the student to be a good speaker and a good man. Its long-range purpose was *to provide the state with capable public servants.*

1. **CHARACTER TRAINING.** Although Rome was wealthy and powerful, Quintilian foresaw the possibility of the degradation of the nation brought about through excesses of luxury and idleness and by the fading of those virtues which had made the old republic strong. Accepting Cate's concept that an orator must be morally good, Quintilian stressed the importance of *self discipline and moral integrity* as aims of education.

2. **STATE WELFARE.** The future orator will influence the welfare of the state. He must be made aware of the social problems, the social feelings and the social consequences of government.

3. <u>SERVICE TO THE STATE.</u> Education ought not to serve ornamental purposes. *The speech of the orator* should be persuasive rather than merely elegant. Education should prepare the orator to *live an effective life of service to the state*.

4. <u>EFFECTIVE SPEECH.</u> The man who could speak persuasively in a time when most men were handicapped by a lack of books, could influence the course of action taken by the state. A man of character who spoke effectively was of enormous value to the state.

PRINCIPLES OF EDUCATION. Some of the following *principles pertaining to teaching* influenced all the subsequent western theorists in education:

1. <u>READINESS.</u> Children ought not to be introduced to subject material until they arrive at *a degree of maturity* which will guarantee success.

2. <u>INDIVIDUAL DIFFERENCES.</u> Each child proceeds at a different pace. There are differences in children's physical and intellectual capabilities which the teacher should take into account.

3. <u>REWARDS.</u> Quintillian advocates *elimination of punishment from the educational scene.* Rewards are better than punishments to promote learning.

4. <u>INTEREST AND MOTIVATION.</u> The wise teacher will make his lessons as pleasurable as possible for the students. This approach will heighten interest and encourage persistence in learning. *Application to learning cannot be forced.*

5. <u>RELATING LEARNING TO THE PRESENT.</u> Quintilian suggests that the content of lessons should, where possible, be *related to contemporary and practical activities.* This teaching technique enhances student interest. Current issues of interest to the young orator should be the basis of the cases assigned for argument.

6. <u>SOCIALIZATION.</u> Public education is superior to private tutoring because it provides opportunities for future citizens to learn how to relate to each other.

ROMAN CONTRIBUTIONS TO EDUCATION

INTELLECTUAL CONTRIBUTIONS. Although the intellectual contributions Rome made to civilization were less original than those of Greece, they were of substantial value. Rome's *legal system, principles of government administration, and language* influenced the development of all the western countries, including their educational development. When the barbarian hordes conquered the Roman empire, the Christian Church became the repository of Roman learning. The Church, itself organized in a way that was similar to Roman governmental organization, preserved Roman laws and the Roman language and literature into modern times.

SCHOOL ORGANIZATION. Rome's organization of its schools set a pattern which western countries have followed.

1. <u>STATE CONTROL.</u>

    a. <u>State Approval.</u> Schools were built only with the Emperor's approval.

    b. <u>Salaries.</u> Teacher's salaries were paid by the state.

    c. <u>Uniform Curriculum.</u> Schools throughout Rome were standardized as to curriculum.

    d. <u>Appointments.</u> Teachers were appointed by the state.

2. <u>SCHOOL SYSTEM.</u> The Roman school system endured in Western Europe. The *Cathedral* and *Monastic* schools of Medieval Europe, as well as the universities

which grew out of them, *retained the subject matter that Rome borrowed from Greece:*

   a. Grammar
   b. Rhetoric
   c. Dialogue
   d. Mathematics
   e. Astronomy
   f. Music
   g. Philosophy.

LATIN LANGUAGE. The Latin language remained the *exclusive language of scholarship* in western Europe until the seventeenth century. Until recent times, Latin held an important place in the curriculum of Western *secondary* education. Aelius Donatus and Caesariensis Priscianus were Roman grammarians who contributed substantially to the study of Latin.

DONATUS

LIFE. The following facts are known about the life of Donatus:

1. **PLACE AND TIME.** He *lived in Rome* during the fourth century A.D.
2. **TEACHER.** He was the *teacher of Saint Jerome.*
3. **WRITER.** He *authored commentaries* on Terrence and Virgil.
4. **WORK.** He compiled the *"Ars Grammatica."*

ARS GRAMMATICA. The Ars Grammatica is divided into:
1. **ARS MINOR.** A *fourteen page* treatise for children dealing with the *parts of speech.* It is catechetical in form. The *terminology and definition* of the *parts of speech* is still in *use today.*
2. **ARS MAIOR.** A longer advanced text on grammar.

INFLUENCE. The Latin grammar of Donatus became the *major text in grammar for almost a thousand years* after his death. Since a knowledge of Latin grammar was the gateway to higher learning during the Middle Ages, the Ars Grammatica became an important text. So universal was the use of this work, that the name Donatus became synonymous with any basic textbook.

PRISCIAN

LIFE. The following facts are known about the life of Priscian:

1. **TIME.** He lived during the end of the fifth and start of the sixth century.
2. **NATIONALITY.** He was a native of Asia Minor, probably Caesarea in Mauretania.
3. **WORK.** He was author of *Institutiones Grammaticae.*

THE INSTITUTIONES. This work is a systematic exposition of Latin grammar. Down the subsequent centuries, when the study of Latin was imperative for scholarship, this work was usually studied after the Ars Minor of Donatus. The work is divided into eighteen books dealing with sounds, word building, inflections and syntax.

5 | EARLY CHRISTIAN EDUCATION

INTRODUCTION. *The teachings of Jesus Christ* spread throughout Western civilization through the efforts of the Christian Church. This teaching influenced every aspect of Western culture. The *Christian doctrine* emphasized:

1. <u>LOVE.</u> A doctrine of love required all men to love God and his neighbor.
2. <u>FATHER.</u> God is the Father of all mankind. He is not merely the creator and law-giver, but a personal and loving God.
3. <u>EQUALITY.</u> All men are equal before God.
4. <u>DESTINY.</u> Man lives on earth in order to merit by his faith and good life an eternal destiny with God in paradise.
5. <u>SPIRITUAL NATURE AND REDEMPTION.</u> Human nature is deprived of the super-natural life because of the sin of Adam. Through the redeeming merits of Christ, the human soul is enabled to live spiritually with God when the human being affirms his faith in Christ.

IMPLICATIONS FOR EDUCATION. The following points indicate the *applications of Christian doctrine to early, church-oriented, education:*

1. <u>AIM.</u> The major purpose of education is to enable man *to live a holy life* in order to achieve eternal union with God.
2. <u>METHOD.</u> It was accepted that the doctrines of Christianity were *absolutely true*. There was no room for questioning the validity of Christ's teachings. Therefore the following methods were employed in the early catechetical and monastic schools:

   a. <u>Question and Answer.</u> Unlike the Socratic dialogue in which the teacher would ask questions in search of truth, the Christian teacher asked a question and waited for the *correct response.*
   b. <u>Lecture.</u> The teacher would speak about the interpretations of Christian doctrine in order to inform his students of the truth as seen by the Church.
   c. <u>Moral Exhortation.</u> The examples of Christ, the martyrs, and the saints were re-lated to encourage the student to imitate their moral behavior.

3. <u>CONTENT.</u> *Reading and writing were important* for the future teacher of Christian doctrine. The faithful Christian had to understand the meaning of the Church doctrine and be able to participate in religious worship. The early Christian writers often were *educated in the literature of the pagan past.* They deplored this litera-ture as a possible source of seduction for the Christian. *The Scriptures, the writings of the Church Fathers and stories of the saints and martyrs* made up the bulk of the reading material they presented to students.

EARLY CHRISTIAN SCHOOLS

TYPES. The early Christian schools were divided into three types:

1. <u>SCHOOL FOR CATECHUMENS.</u> This school provided *possible converts* with information in the dogma and moral tenets of the Christian faith. Instruction was offered in the prayers and scriptures of the church.
2. <u>SCHOOL FOR CATECHISTS.</u> The second type of school trained the *future teachers of Christian doctrine*. The early Christian Church was intensely aggressive in its search for converts. The catechist was taught doctrine in order to refute pagan arguments.
3. <u>CATHEDRAL SCHOOLS.</u> *Education of the clergy* was the purpose of these schools. The curriculum stressed advance knowledge of *scripture and doctrine, ritual and speech,* as well as of *grammar, literature, geometry, history and philosophy.*

EARLY SCHOOLS OF CHRISTIAN THOUGHT

INTRODUCTION. The early centuries of Christian growth were characterized by viewpoints which stemmed from specific schools. These schools were the *School of Alexandria* and the *School of Antioch.*

THE SCHOOL OF ALEXANDRIA. This school was founded by Clement and Origen. The important points of emphasis were:

1. <u>THE CONTEMPLATIVE MOVEMENT.</u> In interpreting scripture, there was a tendency to search for the hidden mystical meanings which might lead to a contemplation of God.
2. <u>THE PHILOSOPHY OF PLATO.</u> The Platonic emphasis upon eternal ideas and the spiritual nature of man was adopted.
3. <u>DIVINITY OF CHRIST AND UNITY OF GOD.</u> This school stressed the divine nature of Christ, often at the expense of his humanity. Because of the oneness of God, the divine nature of Christ was thought by some to be a manifestation of the one God.

THE SCHOOL OF ANTIOCH. This school was founded by Lucianus and Dorotheus. The important points of emphasis which distinguish this school were:

1. <u>RESEARCH.</u> They pursued a *realistic* search for the more *liberal* meaning of the scripture.
2. <u>ANALYSIS.</u> They used the *philosophy of Aristotle* in a careful and logical analysis of doctrine. There was a tendency to rely more on reason than upon the traditional teachings among some of the writers of this school.
3. <u>HUMANITY.</u> There was a tendency to stress *the humanity of Christ.*

EARLY CHRISTIAN TEACHERS

ORIGEN

LIFE OF ORIGEN.

1. <u>EARLY YEARS.</u> Origen was born in *185 A.D.* in Alexandria, Egypt.

    a. <u>Family.</u> His parents were *devout Christians.*
    b. <u>Education.</u> His father taught him both *literature and scripture.*
    c. <u>Persecution.</u> His father was taken during the persecution of Severus.
    d. <u>Advice.</u> Origen encouraged his father to *endure martyrdom.*

2. **TEACHER.** During the persecution of Severus, Origen took over the responsibility of the direction of the *Didascalia* (the moral and disciplinary laws of the Church) at the age of eighteen.

    a. <u>Educating Others.</u> Bishop Demetrius appointed Origen teacher of the *catechetical school* in Alexandria in 203 A.D.
    b. <u>Students.</u> Origen taught many converts who were subsequently martyred.
    c. <u>Educating Himself.</u> After the persecutions, Origen *continued his own education* in 210 A.D. in order to improve his teaching. He studied the following *philosophies:*

        (1) <u>Eclecticism.</u> He studied Eclecticism with the philosopher Saccas.
        (2) <u>Neo-Platonism.</u>
        (3) <u>Pythagorianism.</u>

    d. <u>Travels.</u> Origen travelled through *Rome, Greece and the Middle East.* He began his writings about 212 A.D.
    e. <u>Works.</u> Origen was the *author of thousands of short writings,* many of which are now lost.
    f. <u>Purpose.</u> His major purpose was the development of *Christian character* in his students. They had to *know the scriptures* as well as have *secular learning.*

3. <u>ORDAINED YEARS.</u>

    a. <u>Work.</u> Between 220 and 230 A.D., Origen, not yet an ordained priest, wrote his most famous theological work, the *"De Principiis."*
    b. <u>Reputation.</u> He was renowned throughout the Mediterranean world by 230 A.D.
    c. <u>Ordination.</u> The Bishops of Caesarea and Jerusalem ordained him a priest about 230 A.D.
    d. <u>Heretic.</u> Bishop Demetrius *forbade him to teach* in Alexandria in 231 A.D. A synod then claimed that *Origen was guilty of heresy* on trinitarian matters in his De Principiis. These findings were upheld by another Roman synod.
    e. <u>New School.</u> Origen *left Alexandria* to establish a new theological school in *Caesarea, Palestine.*
    f. <u>Students.</u> Origen taught at his school of higher education in theology for twenty years, attracting some of *the most talented Christians* of the third century.
    g. <u>Imprisoned.</u> During the persecutions of the Emperor Decius, Origen was imprisoned and tortured.
    h. <u>Death.</u> Released from prison, Origen *died* two years later at Tyre, about the year 255 A.D.

EDUCATIONAL IMPORTANCE OF ORIGEN

IMPORTANCE. Origen marks the beginning of *Christian educational practices* which were to continue for a thousand years. Some of the important facts are:

1. **HIGHER EDUCATION.** The schools of Alexandria and Caesarea were schools of higher education which *developed through the work of Origen.*
2. **LIBERAL ARTS.** Origen affirmed the necessity of *secular education* through the study of the liberal arts *in addition to theological study.*
3. **TEACHER PREPARATION.** The Greek and Roman educational system demanded only knowledge and skill at logical thinking from their teachers. The early Christian teacher had to be *orthodox* above all. The Christian teacher studied secular philosophy in order to refute more effectively pagan thought. The Church demanded a degree of *moral excellence* in the character of the Christian teacher. This teacher was expected *to teach as much by example as by word.*

THE BEGINNING OF THE MONASTIC SCHOOLS

JEROME

INTRODUCTION. The monastic schools, which arose in *large numbers during the sixth century,* had their beginnings two centuries earlier in schools like that of *Jerome in Bethlehem.*

LIFE OF JEROME.

1. **EARLY LIFE.**
   a. **Birth.** Jerome was born at Stridon, near Venice, Italy, in 347 A.D.
   b. **Family.** His parents were wealthy Christians.
   c. **Schooling.** Between the ages of twelve and eighteen, Jerome studied the Greek and Latin classics in Rome.
   d. **Baptism.** He was baptized by Pope Liberius in 365 A.D.
   e. **Higher Education.** He studied theology and asceticism with the monks at Aquilea until 374 A.D.
   f. **Travels.** He travelled to Antioch and lived in the nearby desert of Chalcis the life of a solitary monk studying Hebrew and Scripture.
   g. **Ordination.** He was ordained a priest in Antioch by Bishop Paulinus.

2. **MIDDLE YEARS.**
   a. **Return.** Jerome returned to Rome at the request of Pope Damasus, in 382 A.D., to write a new *translation of the Bible.*
   b. **Position.** Jerome was appointed *Papal secretary.*
   c. **Friction.** He *antagonized the clergy* by critizing their luxurious living.
   d. **Scandal.** A scandal arose, in which evil was imputed to *his relationship with a small group of wealthy women* whom he taught asceticism.
   e. **Decides to Leave.** After the election of Pope Siricius, the talk of *scandal increased* to the point that Jerome became determined to leave Rome.
   f. **Palestine.** He moved to Palestine in 385 A.D. He *established a monastery and monastic school in Bethlehem.*
   g. **Paula.** The widow Paula, who had been in Jerome's circle of Roman women, *joined Jerome in Bethlehem* where she established a monastery for women.

3. **THE MONASTERY.**
   a. **Daily Life.** Jerome passed his remaining years quietly as a teacher and writer.
   b. **School.** His school attracted many youths.

c. His Teaching. His students affirmed that he was an *inspiring teacher*, who explained abstruse matters with great *clarity*.

d. Writings. *His writings were many and varied.* He wrote translations, commentaries, histories and controversies.

e. Death. *He died in 420 A.D.*, at the age of seventy-three.

EDUCATIONAL IMPORTANCE OF JEROME. Jerome *stressed the ascetical and moral objectives* of education at the expense of the earthly concerns of man. This influenced subsequent Christian monastic schools. As a result, *scientific knowledge suffered* for centuries to come. However, Christian emphasis upon *the equality of man* in the eyes of God led to the principle of *universal education*, which developed slowly through many centuries. The duty of love as a necessity for all Christians led to schools that value *cooperation* rather than force.

SAINT AUGUSTINE

INTRODUCTION. Saint Augustine was the greatest of the Christian writers. He exerted immense influence on the Church and his educational views were adopted and followed for many centuries.

LIFE OF AUGUSTINE.

1. BOYHOOD.

a. Birth. He was born at *Tagaste*, in North Africa, on November 13, 354 A.D.

b. Family. His parents were comfortable *middle-class people*. His father, Patricius, was a pagan and his mother, *Monica*, was a *devout Christian*.

c. Schooling. He was educated in the *Latin grammar school of Madaura* and the *school of rhetoric in Carthage*.

d. Religion. He adopted the Manichaean faith.

2. TEACHER. Positions in Augustine's teaching career were:

a. Grammar. He taught in the Latin grammar school at Tagaste.

b. Rhetoric. He opened a school of rhetoric at Carthage in 374 A.D.

c. Rome. He sailed for Rome and taught rhetoric there.

d. Milan. He accepted a professorship in rhetoric at Milan.

3. CONVERT. Augustine became converted to Christianity.

a. Baptism. Bishop Ambrose baptized Augustine and his son, Adeodatus, in 387 A.D.

b. Tagaste. Following the death of his mother, Augustine returned to Tagaste in 388 A.D.

c. Monastic Order. He established a small monastic order that subsequently developed into the Augustine order.

d. Ordination. Augustine was ordained a priest by the Bishop of Hippo in 391 A.D.

4. BISHOP.

a. Consecration. Augustine became the *Bishop of Hippo* in 396 A.D.

b. His Great Works. He wrote the *Confessions*, the *Trinity* and *The City of God*.

These are most important writings.

c. **Other Writings.** He engaged in *polemical writings*, wrote *scriptural commentaries* and guided the Church in doctrinal matters.

d. **Death.** He died in August, 430 A.D., during the Vandal siege of Hippo.

THE EDUCATIONAL IMPORTANCE OF ST. AUGUSTINE

AIMS OF EDUCATION. Augustine continued the Christian emphasis upon the future life of man, stressing that this life is merely a preparation for the life to come. A man is educated when his moral character and understanding of his faith are developed to their fullest potential.

PRINCIPLES OF EDUCATION. The following concepts describe *Augustinian thought regarding education:*

1. **OPPOSES SENSE EXPERIENCE.** Man must realize that the senses deceive him. Truth and goodness exist only in God. Man arrives at genuine knowledge and virtue after he controls his senses and frees his spirit *to intuit God* by reason of the supernatural life. This life is given to man when he is baptized.

2. **TRUTH IS ABSOLUTE.** Truth is not discovered through experimentation. It is found *within the Catholic Church alone.* This truth is eternal and unchanging.

3. **AUTHORITARIAN.** Truth is defined by the Church. The individual must accept obediently whatever the Church declares as truth. *The individual is not free* to follow whatever direction his reason takes him.

4. **DISCIPLINE.** Although Augustine deplored cruelty, he asserted that punishment is necessary for the child to learn. Because of original sin, the pupil is inclined toward evil. He *must be restrained and punished physically* when it becomes apparent that his evil inclinations are not subdued.

5. **CURRICULUM.** The content of the child's education *should include the secular learning of the pagans,* in order to enrich the student's appreciation of sacred scripture. The study of rhetoric, grammar, logic, mathematics, science and philosophy provide a background for the student who intends to arrive at genuine knowledge *in the study of theology.* Augustine was in favor of censoring strictly the literary content of the child's reading, lest the child be turned away from virtue.

THE IMPORTANCE OF AUGUSTINIAN EDUCATIONAL THOUGHT.

1. **UNIVERSAL INFLUENCE.** The writings of Augustine were accepted by the Church and, through the Church, *influenced subsequent educational theory* for over a thousand years.

2. **MORAL STRENGTH.** The moral education of a Europe over-run by barbarians, demanded *a rigorous ethical foundation* in which a civilization could grow and prosper. Augustine contributed to this moral improvement.

3. **RETARDED SCIENTIFIC GROWTH.** Passive acceptance of absolute truths *retarded the free inquiry* necessary for scientific growth. Furthermore, the subordination of secular sciences and philosophy to theology inhibited the freedom of inquiry and exploration necessary to higher education.

6 | MOHAMMEDAN EDUCATION

INTRODUCTION. Education and learning were stimulated in Arabia after the spread of Mohammedanism. The new learning resulted in an *intellectual conflict between the Islamic and Christian philosophers*, thus stimulating western thought.

MOHAMMED

LIFE. These are events worth remembering in the life of Mohammed:

1. <u>BIRTH.</u> Mohammed was born in *570 A.D. at Mecca.*
2. <u>JOB.</u> He worked as a conductor of caravans.
3. <u>MARRIAGE.</u> He married *Khadija, a wealthy widow* fifteen years his senior, in 595 A.D.
4. <u>EDUCATION.</u> Although he was *barely literate,* Mohammed had assimilated *some Jewish and Christian religious doctrine.*
5. <u>THE CALL.</u> About 610 A.D., Mohammed felt that he had been called as a *religious prophet to succeed Christ.* He counted his wife, cousin and nephew among his first converts.
6. <u>PERSECUTION.</u> After three years of secrecy, his followers announced Mohammed's doctrines. This resulted in the persecution of the early Mohammedans *by the authorities of Mecca.*
7. <u>THE FLIGHT.</u> Mohammed fled to Yathrib, which later became known as Medina or "the city" of the prophet. *The hejira or flight is marked as the beginning of the Mohammedan era—July 16, 622 A.D.*
8. <u>NUMEROUS MARRIAGES.</u> Mohammed entered into numerous marriages in order *to solidify his position* among his followers.
9. <u>DICTATOR.</u> After becoming dictator of Medina, he carried on *a successful military campaign against Mecca.*
10. <u>ACHIEVEMENT.</u> At the time of his death on June 7, 632 A.D., Mohammed had subjugated most of Arabia and was preparing an attack upon Syria. His successor was called Caliph (successor of the Prophet), and subsequent Caliphs conquered every nation from the Spanish Pyrenees through North Africa and the Middle East to the borders of India.

MOHAMMEDAN DOCTRINE

DOCTRINE. The Islamic religion, which Mohammed began, taught the following:

1. <u>ALLAH IS ONE.</u> God is One and Universal. There exists *no intermediary* between God and man.
2. <u>MOHAMMED, THE GREATEST PROPHET.</u> Islam accepted the Jewish prophets and regarded Christ as one of those prophets. But *Mohammed,* in the Islam view, *was the last and greatest prophet.*

3. <u>KORAN.</u> The sacred book begun by Mohammed, and written under the guidance of the angel Gabriel, is *the guide of life for all Mohammedans.*
4. <u>MORALITY.</u> The Mohammedan is directed to *pray daily, give to the poor and orphans, observe the fast of Ramadan and make a pilgrimage to Mecca* if possible. He is directed to *avoid eating pork, drinking alcoholic beverages, gambling, idol worship and infanticide.*
5. <u>EQUALITY.</u> All who accept the Islamic faith are *considered equal, regardless of race or nationality.* This doctrine, along with the assurance that those who died fighting for the faith would achieve paradise, helps to account for the rapid spread of the religion.
6. <u>PARADISE OR HELL.</u> Those who observed the faith would be rewarded with *a sensuous paradise after death.* Unbelievers and the faithless are doomed to an afterlife of hell-fire forever.

ISLAMIC EDUCATION

INTRODUCTION. Mohammed praised education and, as a result, *learning flourished in Islamic countries* for three and a half centuries. These countries advanced learning in *medicine, literature, science, philosophy and mathematics.* This learning became the subject material of Western medieval universities. Because the Mohammedans used the invention of *paper* effectively, *large libraries* came into existence in all the major cities of Islam, with a reading populace, trained in the Koran, eagerly consuming the works.

EDUCATION IN ISLAMIC COUNTRIES.

1. <u>BEGINNINGS.</u> Between 750 and 850 A.D., Moslem schools were usually *attached to the mosque* in each city. As wealth increased, *schools were built by private subscription* or with the aid of large donations. These and subsequent schools were characterized by the following:

   a. <u>Intellectual Curiosity.</u> The scholarship was *not limited to theology and religious doctrine.* It extended into every area of human inquiry.
   b. <u>Classical.</u> The Mohammedans *borrowed heavily from classical sources.* The school system and writings of the Greeks were assimilated into their educational organization.
   c. <u>Cultural Assimilation.</u> The cultures of Persia, Greece and India were assimilated and improved upon by the Moslems.

2. <u>GOLDEN AGE.</u> *Between 850 and 1000 A.D.,* the Golden Age of Moslem education, the Mohammedans advanced the study of *medicine, science, mathematics and philosophy.* The numerous translations led to new interpretations of Neo-Platonism and Aristotelianism.

ISLAMIC SCHOLARS

PROMINENT SCHOLARS. Two of Islam's *most important writers* were Avicenna and Averroes.

AVICENNA.

1. <u>TIME.</u> He lived between the years *979 and 1037 A.D.*

2. **POSITION.** He was a prominent and successful *physician.*
3. **PHILOSOPHY.** He was an authority on *Aristotelianism and Neo-Platonism.*
4. **GREAT WORK.** He wrote the *Cannon of Medicine.*

   a. The Cannon is divided into *five books,* treating:

      (1) **Physiology**
      (2) **Pathology**
      (3) **Treatment**
      (4) **Prescriptions**
      (5) **Clinical observations.**

   b. **Translation into Latin.** The Cannon was translated into Latin by Gerard of Cremona in 1187 A.D., and was studied as *the principal text in medicine* in European universities until 1650 A.D.

5. **THE AL SHIFA.** In addition to many treatises, Avicenna authored the *al Shifa.*

   a. **The Book.** The al Shifa is a philosophical work based on *Aristotle's logic, metaphysics, physics and mathematics.*
   b. **Importance.** This represents *Avicenna's most influential work.*

AVERROES. Important facts about Averroes are:

1. **TIME AND PLACE.** He lived *between the years 1126 and 1198 A.D. in Cordova, Spain.*
2. **IMPORTANCE.** He is the *most important Islamic philosopher.*
3. **WORKS.** Many works were written by him on *grammar, astronomy, medicine and philosophy.*
4. **COMMENTARIES.** His commentaries on philosophy *influenced many Western thinkers,* particularly those early philosophers of the University of Paris.
5. **INTERPRETATIONS.** Some of Averroes' *important philosophical interpretations of Aristotle* are the following:

   a. **Universal Soul.** *The active intellect in the human soul is a part of the universal soul.* The active intellect is, therefore, the same in all human beings. It emanates from God, of which it is a part.
   b. **Matter.** Material nature is eternal potentiality. It had no beginning in time and will have no end.
   c. **Destiny of Man.** Man has *no eternal destiny. His individuality ceases at death.* The active intellect, which is the spiritual life force within him, is impersonal, having emanated from God. This *impersonal force continues after the individual personality dies.*
   d. **Determinism.** Man has *no free choice.* His actions are determined by his nature.
   e. **Theological and Philosophical Conflict.** Averroes believed that *contradictory propositions could exist simultaneously* in theology and philosophy.

7 | EDUCATION DURING THE MIDDLE AGES

INTRODUCTION. *The period between the end of the Roman Empire and the year 1500 is known as the Middle Ages.* The Germanic tribes, under pressure from the Asiatic Huns, moved into the empire. Eventually they overran and conquered the empire. These *tribes accepted the culture of Rome and Greece*, which included the Christian religion. In the East, the conquest of the Moslems limited the power of the Eastern Church, so that the Roman Church emerged as the dominant influence in Western Europe during these centuries.

THE EARLY MIDDLE AGES. By the end of the sixth century, *education had dwindled to a few monastic schools.* What learning remained was preserved in laboriously copied scrolls in monastic libraries. Much of the Greek learning, including all Aristotelian works, were lost for centuries to the West.

SOCIAL AND POLITICAL BACKGROUND. The period of time between the Papal rule of Gregory I, at the beginning of the seventh century, and the rule of Pope Gregory VII, in the eleventh century, is characterized by the following important events:

1. **THE GROWTH OF FEUDALISM.** Feudal origins are traceable to both Latin and Germanic customs. *The patronage system,* by which Roman citizens achieved security and protection from the local noble in return for services, was similar to the practice of *Comitatus* among the Germans. When the strong centralized governments found themselves powerless to protect their citizens in the face of barbarian invasions and banditry, individuals turned to the local noble for assistance.

2. **FEUDAL SOCIETY.** The *class structure* under feudalism is divided into:

   a. **King and Nobility.** The nobles received land from the king in return for a promise to support the king militarily when the need arose.
   b. **Clergy.** The clergy was divided into the following:

      (1) **Secular.** The secular clergy *operated in secular society* and were subject to bishops. The bishops frequently held land in the name of the king. Bishops were considered nobles.
      (2) **Regular.** The designation, regular clergy, was derived from the Latin verb "regulare," which means to rule. These clergymen *accepted the rule* of some monastery, living lives of poverty, chastity and obedience *within the confines of the monastery.* This movement began with the rule of St. Benedict. Benedict established the first Italian monastery in 520 A.D.

   c. **Peasants and Serfs.** Since there were few cities in Medieval Europe, *common men lived agricultural lives* on the land of some noble. Their condition limited them to lives of ignorance, superstition and hardship. The man who was free of the land was called *a freeman*. Those attached to the land, i.e. unable to leave the estate, were termed "serfs."

3. **THE GROWTH OF PAPAL POWER.** *Pope Gregory the Great (590-604) initiated Papal dominance*. His successful defense of Rome against the barbarian Lombards provided the beginning of Papal temporal rule. Gregory initiated the system of taxation, by which the Papacy was supported. Subsequently, the *Carolingian Kings increased Papal power* and influence by:

a. Costs. They acted as underwriters for the costs of country parishes.
b. Laws. They passed laws taxing the people for the support of the Church.
c. Territory. They gave the Pope the territory later called the Papal States.
d. Protection. They protected the Papal lands from encroachment.

EDUCATION IN THE EARLY MIDDLE AGES. During the early Middle Ages, *education was characterized by:*

1. **MONASTIC SCHOOLS.** The schools were *originally designed to train the clergy*. These schools retained the Roman system. The Monastic school existed for boys vowed to a monastic life. Boys were accepted in the *outer school* to be educated for secular life. These boys were educated in *the seven liberal arts of the trivium and the quadrivium*.

   a. Trivium. The trivium contained the following *three subjects:*

     (1) Grammar. The reason for the study of grammar was to enable a man to *express himself with clarity* in speech and writing.
     (2) Rhetoric. Rhetoric consists of the *rules of* effective written and spoken *communication*.
     (3) Logic. The *rules of correct thinking* are termed logic.

   b. Quadrivium. The quadrivium contained the following *four subjects:*

     (1) Arithmetic. It was believed that the study of numbers might help the student understand the hidden meanings contained in the Scriptures. It was not until the twelfth century that mathematics improved in the West with the *introduction of arabic numberals*.
     (2) Geometry. The study of *Euclid* was unknown in Europe until the twelfth century.
     (3) Music. Early music was associated with the *Church ritual*.
      (a) Schools of Music. A few schools of music were established to train talented boys in vocal music for the Papal choirs.
     (4) Astronomy. *Astronomy was restricted* by the lack of method, of mathematics and of instruments. It was associated with the superstition of *astrology*.

2. **IRISH MONASTIC EDUCATION.** When the Saxons conquered England, Christianity was virtually destroyed. Ireland was spared this invasion. Converted to Christianity by *St. Patrick* in the middle of the fifth century, Irish monasticism grew. Irish missionaries were sent to convert and educate Scotland and England. They established a monastic community at *Iona, Scotland*, in 530 A.D. Subsequently, the Irish sent missionaries to the continent of Europe. The *monastery of St. Gall* in Switzerland

was established by Irish monks. This monastery became one of the centers for *musical learning* in Europe. Irish monastic education ceased with the Viking invasions of Ireland in the tenth and eleventh centuries. It regained its former vigor after assimilating the defeated Danes, and continued until it was suppressed by Henry VIII of England.

3. **ENGLISH MONASTIC EDUCATION.** The principal centers for education and Christianity in England were the monasteries at *Jarrow, York, Malmesbury and Canterbury. Aldhelm*, the first Saxon poet, was educated by the Irish monks of Malmesbury. The *two most important figures in education* in Saxon England were:

   a. <u>The Venerable Bede.</u> Bede spent his life at Jarrow in the North of England. He is famous as an *historian and a scripture scholar* and as the author of text books on arithmetic, handwriting, the exegesis of scripture and astronomy.

   b. <u>Alcuin.</u> Regarding *the life and the contributions of Alcuin to education*, these are the points to note:

      (1) <u>Birth.</u> He was born *near London in 735 A.D.*
      (2) <u>Monk.</u> He entered *the monastery of York* where he remained for thirty years as a student, teacher and abbot.
      (3) <u>France.</u> On leaving the primitive North of England, he went to the *Palace School of the Emperor Charlemagne at Aix-la-Chapelle.*
      (4) <u>Importance.</u> He became a central figure in the *educational reforms of Charlemagne* during the twelve years he taught in the Palace School.
      (5) <u>Death.</u> He became the abbot of the monastery of *Tours*, and died there in *804 A.D.*

4. **EDUCATIONAL REFORMS OF CHARLEMAGNE.** Charlemagne was a great patron of Latin education. He encouraged learning among his clergy and nobility. Here are some aspects of *educational conditions* in the Empire of Charlemagne:

   a. <u>Cathedral Schools.</u> These schools existed for the training of boys in reading and singing for Church services and in copying manuscripts.

      (1) <u>Discipline.</u> Discipline was *severe in the extreme.* Boys unable to memorize or apply themselves were physically punished.
      (2) <u>Liberal Arts.</u> The curriculum comprised *the trivium and quadrivium* of the liberal arts. Theology was studied only in the monastic schools by future priests.
      (3) <u>Method.</u> The usual method of teaching was *by question and answer*, the learner being expected to provide the correct response.

   b. <u>Monastic Schools.</u> *The Palace School* was their model. Although the Palace School had existed prior to Charlemagne, it was this emperor who placed the School in such high esteem that through the efforts of Alcuin it became a *force in the education of Europe. Alcuin achieved the following in the School:*

      (1) <u>Classics.</u> Classical *Latin culture was restored.*
      (2) <u>Influence.</u> He trained the future *teachers, writers and scholars* of Europe for a hundred years to come.
      (3) <u>Texts.</u> A *uniformity of Christian worship* was made possible by the provision of copied texts for ritual, scripture and music.

LATER MIDDLE AGES

INTRODUCTION. The period between the eleventh and fifteenth centuries witnessed the full fruition of those forces that had been gathering strength since the seventh century. Theology, philosophy, the fine arts, architecture and law were cultivated to new and greater refinements. The twelfth and thirteenth centuries are particularly renowned for their productivity. *The later Middle Ages in Western Europe were characterized by:*

1. <u>**INTERNATIONALISM**</u>
2. <u>**UNITY OF FAITH**</u>
3. <u>**STRONG PAPACY**</u>
4. <u>**SUBORDINATION TO AUTHORITY**</u>
5. <u>**INSTITUTIONALISM**</u>
6. <u>**GROWTH OF CITIES**</u>
7. <u>**CRUSADES**</u>
8. <u>**RELIGIOUS ORDERS**</u>
9. <u>**UNIVERSITIES**</u>
10. <u>**UNIVERSAL LATIN LANGUAGE**</u>
11. <u>**PHILOSOPHY OF SCHOLASTICISM.**</u>

POLITICAL BACKGROUND.

1. <u>**PAPAL REFORM.**</u> The movement to free the Papacy from corruption and secular influence began at the monastery of *Cluny*, was implemented by the election of the monk Hildebrand as *Pope Gregory VII*.
2. <u>**PAPAL SUPREMACY.**</u> The struggle between the Papacy and the emperors, having been started to free the Papacy from lay investiture of religious offices, ended with *the Pope as the most powerful figure in Europe.* Pope Innocent III considered himself the intermediate between God and man in temporal as well as spiritual affairs.
3. <u>**NATIONALISM.**</u> While the Popes were engaged in their struggle with the German emperors of the Holy Roman Empire, *the kings of France and England* consolidated their national positions.
4. <u>**AVIGNON PAPACY.**</u> Between 1309 and 1376 the popes fell *under the control of the French king.* The Papacy was moved to Avignon in France. This period ended in a schism lasting from 1377-1417. The Council of Constance ended the schism with the election of a new pope in Rome.
5. <u>**RELIGIOUS UNREST.**</u> The Albigensians and the Waldensians were heretical religious sects which revolted against the established Christian dogma emanating from Rome. *John Wycliffe* in England and *John Huss* on the Continent attacked abuses in the Church. Generally, however, this was *a period of great orthodoxy.* Heresy was ruthlessly suppressed.
6. <u>**CRUSADES.**</u> Pope Urban II called the First Crusade in 1095 in order to regain the Holy Land from the Moslems. During the Middle Ages *eight crusades* were called against the Moslems, with the following results:

   a. <u>Military Failure.</u> They *failed to defeat Moslem rule* in the Holy Land.
   b. <u>Trade.</u> The *Mediterranean* was opened to trade.
   c. <u>Economics.</u> They *impoverished the nobles* and *strengthened* the rule of the *kings.*
   d. <u>Unity.</u> *Christianity in Europe* was further unified.

   e. <u>New Influences.</u> *Moslem culture and learning* were introduced into Europe.

   f. <u>Lost Works.</u> Many *lost Greek masterpieces* including *the writings of Aristotle,* which had been preserved in Moslem schools, were rediscovered.

EDUCATION IN THE LATER MIDDLE AGES

EDUCATION. Some noteworthy points of education in the later Middle Ages were:

1. <u>BEGINNINGS AND GROWTH OF THE UNIVERSITIES</u>
2. <u>DEVELOPMENT OF SCHOLASTICISM</u>
3. <u>RISE OF GREAT SCHOLARS AND TEACHINGS OF THE CHURCH.</u>

THE UNIVERSITY

BEGINNINGS. The university in the Middle Ages began during *the later part of the twelfth century.* The facts are the following:

1. <u>MOSLEM INFLUENCE.</u> With the introduction of Moslem and Greek learning through translations, *there arose an interest in classical learning.* The writings on Aristotle gave rise to new interpretations of theological doctrine.
2. <u>THEOLOGICAL DISPUTATION.</u> Intellectual interest in theology was stimulated by the theological controversy regarding the nature of universals. This controversy arose as a result of *a conflict between Platonic and Aristotelian thought.* The student required additional knowledge in logic and debating to take part in the theological disputes.
3. <u>ADVANCED TRAINING IN THE PROFESSIONS.</u> With the growth of populations and cities, the need became greater for *highly-trained professionals in law and medicine.*
4. <u>INFORMAL BEGINNINGS.</u> Teachers and students possessing a common interest *came together to lecture, to learn and to debate.*

THE EARLY UNIVERSITY. These practices were typical in the early universities:

1. <u>UNIVERSITAS.</u> The early teachers and students found it necessary to *incorporate themselves for their own protection.* The University of Paris was one of the first to be incorporated. This institution's charter from the king, obtained through a petition, protected it from interference or domination by outside secular or Church authorities.
2. <u>EARLY UNIVERSITIES.</u> The University of *Paris* offered degrees *in the arts.* Its initial interest was in the area of theology. The University of *Bologna* specialized *in law,* and the University of *Salerno in medicine.*
3. <u>DEGREES.</u> The medieval university offered degrees. The degree of *Bachelor of Arts* provided one with the right to become a candidate for higher degrees. The *Master's* and the higher *Doctor's* degrees were given by the university to those who demonstrated their scholarship and learning ability through *the defense of a thesis.*
4. <u>RIGHTS AND PRIVILEGES.</u> The degree given by the university provided the recipient with the right *to practice his profession or to teach* anywhere in Europe. *Additional privileges* were:

   a. <u>Taxes.</u> The holder of a degree was *not subject to taxation.*

   b. <u>Conscription.</u> He was *not liable* for military service.

c. <u>Law.</u> A degree meant *freedom from the jurisdiction* of civil courts.

5. <u>TEACHING.</u> The word "doctor" is derived from the latin word *docere* meaning "to teach." Teaching in the university took the following forms:

    a. <u>Lecture.</u> The master or doctor would lecture to his students by *reading from a book which he had written*. This method was necessitated by the lack of books during the Middle Ages. As he read, he would comment upon his text to clarify or to add to the information.

        (1) <u>Ordinary Lecture.</u> The lecture *delivered by the master or doctor* was called the ordinary lecture.

        (2) <u>Extraordinary Lecture.</u> The extraordinary lecture was delivered *by an advanced student who repeated an earlier lecture* of the master or doctor for the benefit of those who were unable to take notes upon it.

    b. <u>Disputation.</u> Debates were *organized to present opposing intellectual positions.* These debates followed the rules of logic set down by Aristotle in the Organon.

6. <u>ADMINISTRATION.</u> The administrative organization of the early university consisted of:

    a. <u>Rector.</u> Initially the Rector was subject to the Chancellor of the cathedral school. However, the Rector was *the chief administrator of the university*. He was elected to office by the Deans and Counselors of students. In time the Rector became superior to the Chancellor. In Jesuit institutions the role of Chancellor became that of curriculum director and dispenser of degrees.

    b. <u>Dean.</u> *The senior member of each of the faculties of Law, Theology, Medicine and the Arts* would be named Dean. The Dean operated as the final authority on matters pertaining to intellectual discipline.

    c. <u>Faculty.</u> The masters and doctors were *organized into four faculties*, according to their specializations: Law, Theology, Medicine and the Arts.

7. <u>THE COLLEGE.</u> The early university comprised only a few rented buildings in the city. Eventually the university acquired its own buildings. The college was no more than a hotel for undergraduate scholars at the beginning. As time progressed a master would preside over the college. This master imposed regulations governing the academic and moral behavior of the youthful students. *All degrees were issued by the university. In England the colleges became autonomous* to the extent that Oxford and Cambridge became communities of separate colleges. This condition did not exist in continental Europe.

8. <u>THE CURRICULUM.</u> The undergraduate curriculum followed the seven liberal arts contained in the trivium and quadrivium. There was heavy emphasis upon learning the Latin language to provide the student with the ability to continue his specialization in graduate education. All lectures were conducted in Latin. During *the thirteenth century, the Pope fixed the curricula for the four faculties*. There existed a heavy reliance upon Moslem sources translated into Latin.

SCHOLASTICISM

GENERAL FEATURES. The major reason for the Papal support of universities was to strengthen the Faith. During the later Middle Ages, the *religious system of thought* which is termed *scholasticism* arose chiefly through the writings of *St. Thomas Aquinas.* Some *important features of scholasticism* are:

1. **RELIGIOUS PHILOSOPHY OF MAN.** The nature and destiny of man is interpreted in the religious sense. However, an effort is made to support this religious interpretation *through reason.* It is assumed that the logic of reasoned propositions regarding man *would compel* the intellectual assent of the hearer.
2. **PHILOSOPHY "THE HANDMAIDEN" OF THEOLOGY.** When reason fails to answer any of the ultimate questions of reality, man must rely upon faith. *Reason can support what man already knows by faith.* Man can never hope to find solutions to the ultimate questions by reason alone. It is for these reasons that philosophy, which is dependent upon reason, is subordinated to theology.
3. **RATIONALISM.** In the philosophy of Aquinas there is careful attention given to the rules of formal logic. Proceeding from the self-evident principles of being, identity and contradition, *he relies upon the deductive processes of rational analysis to arrive at truth.*
4. **EDUCATIONAL IMPORTANCE.** Scholasticism is *the official philosophy of the Roman Catholic Church.* In the encyclical "Aeterni Patris" of 1879, Pope Leo XIII raised this system of thought to a place of honor in the Church. It is the theoretical foundation of the Catholic system of education from elementary school through college.

IMPORTANT SCHOLARS

INTRODUCTION. Some important scholars and teachers of this period were:

1. **ABELARD.** Abelard was important to education because:

   a. **His Renown.** He attracted students from all over Europe to Paris, and therefore was instrumental in *beginning the University of Paris.*
   b. **Influence.** He emphasized *logic and argumentation* in his teaching method. This approach influenced later scholasticism.
   c. **His New Approach.** He taught that it is necessary to *doubt all truths* and then to *search for the logical evidence* that would verify the truth. This notion was foreign to the Middle Ages. However, it influenced subsequent thinkers.
   d. **The Classics.** *He revived an interest in classical thinkers.* The arguments which he presented made use of pagan classical sources as well as Christian quotations.

2. **ALBERT THE GREAT.** Albert the Great was important to education because:

   a. **Teacher.** He was the *teacher of Thomas Aquinas.*
   b. **Philosophy.** He was one of the *first in western Europe to adopt the philosophy of Aristotle.*
   c. **Adaptation.** He began *the systematic adaptation of Aristotle to Christian thought.*

4. **THOMAS AQUINAS.**

   a. **Status.** This Dominican monk was *the most important scholar and thinker* in the Middle Ages.
   b. **Influence.** His philosophy represents *the official philosophy of the Roman Catholic Church.*

c. **Works.** He was the author of *Summa Contra Gentiles, Summa Theologiae, Commentaries upon Aristotle, and The Book of Sentences.* He also wrote on the Scriptures and on Boethius.

d. **Philosophy of Aquinas.** Some important generalizations regarding the philosophy of Aquinas are:

(1) **Superiority of Faith.** Both *faith and reason* are reliable sources of knowledge. However, faith is superior *because it yields certain knowledge.*

(2) **A Definition of Reason.** *Man is a rational animal.* He possesses a soul and a body. The *soul is the form* of the material body, and *reason constitutes the highest faculty of the soul.*

(3) **The Soul.** The soul is the *principle of life.* It survives bodily death and rejoins the glorified body upon the Final Judgment of man.

(4) **God Is Prime Act.** Man knows the *existence* of God because of the arguments from *motion, efficient causality, necessary and contingent beings, and design and perfection in the universe.*

(5) **The Aim of Mankind.** The *greatest good* for man is the happiness derived from his *union with God.* God is the final end of all beings.

(6) **Virtue.** Virtue consists of *acting in accordance with one's final end.*

(7) **Society.** Man is by nature a *social animal* who must live in society. The ideal government makes possible those circumstances which *allow men to develop their full potentialities and to serve God.*

4. **JOHN DUNS SCOTUS.** John Duns Scotus had highly original points of view for his time:

a. **Influence.** He was a *Scottish Franciscan monk,* important for his influence upon *subsequent English scholars and teachers.*

b. **His Philosophy.** A critic of Aquinas' philosophy, Scotus gave priority to the *faculty of will* in man's soul rather than reason, as Aquinas insisted.

c. **Not a Theorist.** A strong advocate of the *practical purpose of theological study,* he opposed the theoretical explorations of doctrine which engaged the attention of so many medieval theologians.

8 | THE RENAISSANCE AND HUMANISM

INTRODUCTION. With the fall of Constantinople to the Moslems in 1453, *many Byzantine scholars came as refugees to live in Italy.* They brought with them classical scholarship and a practical humanistic outlook regarding education. The literature of this age was modeled after classical Greek and Latin authors. In education, interest in Cicero and Quintillian was reawakened.

SOCIAL BACKGROUND OF RENAISSANCE EDUCATION. Major social forces gave impetus to the development of a new kind of education during the Renaissance. These forces were:

1. <u>HUMANISM.</u> The Renaissance was marked by *a revolt against the asceticism of the Middle Ages.* Social concern focused upon human life rather than spiritual life, upon good living in this life rather than in some future after-life.
2. <u>WEALTH.</u> The social change brought about during this period began in the homes of wealthy merchants and in the palaces of the aristocracy. With the rise of trade and the increase in banking and commercial enterprises, great wealth brought *new luxuries and leisure to the affluent.*
3. <u>EXPLORATION.</u> Foreign trade and mercantile interests led to a spirit of exploration. The great discoveries of *new lands* began during this period.
4. <u>VERNACULAR LANGUAGES.</u> The *development of the Romance Languages* took place during this time. These languages won respect as the vehicles of the literary works of the time.
5. <u>FINE ARTS.</u> The Renaissance was marked by *a resurgence of painting and sculpture.* New interest arose in color and the human figure.
6. <u>INDIVIDUALISM.</u> This age was noteworthy for its regard for the individual. The institutionalism that characterized medieval Europe rapidly was replaced with *a new emphasis upon individual freedom.*

EDUCATION DURING THE RENAISSANCE. The educational changes which occurred during the Renaissance were the following:

1. <u>RISE OF PUBLIC AND PRIVATE SCHOOLS FREE OF ECCLESIASTICAL CONTROL.</u> At the end of the thirteenth century, many independent *cities had control over their own schools.* These schools were taught by *lay teachers.* In *Florence and Milan* lay teachers were organized into guilds. These were the *significant developments* in public and private education free of ecclesiastical influence and control:

   a. <u>Guiding Philosophy.</u> *The philosophy of Aristotle,* which won wide acceptance during the Middle Ages, *favored public education.* The discovery of the "Politics" of Aristotle at the beginning of the Renaissance, provided additional impetus to this form of education.

b. <u>Power Structure.</u> *Imperial powers achieved ascendancy over Papal authority* in temporal affairs. The nobility recognized the great stake which the state has in education.

c. <u>Education for the People.</u> *The Netherlands*, by the end of the fourteenth century, were the first to achieve universal schools and complete literacy among the population of the independent towns. The schools were freed from Church control and were placed under the authority of the local aristocracy.

d. <u>State Education.</u> *An act of the Scottish Parliament in 1496* made education a concern of the state. This was the first legislation which placed education under government control rather than under control of the king alone or of the church.

e. <u>City Schools.</u> The *Burgh Schools in Germany* were city Latin schools which were established by the city council rather than by the ecclesiastical authorities. Teachers were employees of the city.

2. <u>**THE AIM OF EDUCATION.**</u> During the Renaissance the purpose of education became the development of self-realization in a cultured aristocrat. Education was intellectual, cultural, ornamental and practical for the times. *It aimed at developing a whole man to live in a leisured class.*

3. <u>**INTRODUCTION OF CLASSICAL GREEK AND LATIN LITERATURE.**</u> At the beginning of the Middle Ages, the Fathers of the Roman Catholic Church considered pagan literature to be evil in its ability to turn away man's mind from the affairs of Eternity. The Renaissance educator reversed this, stressing the study of classic "pagan" Greek and Latin literature. Renaissance teachers *believed that the Classics provided practical information and guidance in literary style.* The poetic, dramatic and historical literature of classical antiquity was taught in such a way as to reinforce the moral and ethical principles of society.

4. <u>**MORAL EDUCATION.**</u> Almost all of the educational theorists of this time were concerned about character education. However, the Renaissance was a period of moral decadence and degeneration. The emphasis upon individuality and sensuality, the rebellion against the austerity and asceticism of medieval times, and the formalism and ritual in Italian worship rather than a concern with the morality of behavior, led to *the total failure of character education.*

5. <u>**HIGHER EDUCATION.**</u> Theology was replaced in the curriculum of the universities by a subject which combined grammar, literature and rhetoric. Although *Latin classical literature* held the place of honor, *Greek classical literature* was included. Toward the end of the Renaissance, *history and the vernacular languages were introduced.*

6. <u>**LIBERAL ARTS.**</u> The seven liberal arts of the *trivium and quadrivium* were retained. These arts of the free men of leisure in ancient Athens became the means by which the Renaissance man liberated his rational and emotional nature.

7. <u>**LAYMAN REPLACES PRIEST AS TEACHER.**</u> Education had been the exclusive concern of the Church during the Middle Ages. The only schooling that existed took place in monastic and cathedral schools. The teachers were nearly always priests. This situation was changed during the Renaissance. However, *many priests continued to teach in the universities.*

8. <u>**EDUCATION OF WOMEN.**</u> Formal coeducation was *non-existent* during this period. The majority of women had the same low educational status they had during the Middle Ages, trained by their mothers in the home. Toward the end of the Renaissance, it was recognized by some that noble women required some education to prepare them to be successful companions to their educated husbands in court life. *Castiglione* wrote in *"The Book of the Courtier"* that aristocratic *women*

should be tutored in literature, music, drawing, painting, dancing, sports and games.

9. <u>ELEMENTARY EDUCATION.</u> During the first three years of schooling the child learned *reading, writing, arithmetic and drawing.* The language spoken in the school was Latin. The child was taught *Greek and Latin grammar.* There was a heavy reliance upon memory because of the lack of books.

10. <u>SECONDARY EDUCATION.</u> The youth was introduced to *rhetoric* during secondary education. He studied the *rules of composition and was required to write original compositions.* He read *the classical poets and historians.* He practiced *the art of eloquent speech.*

FAMOUS EDUCATORS DURING THE RENAISSANCE. The following were important Renaissance educators:

1. <u>VITTORINO DA FELTRE.</u> Vittorino was the most important educator during the Renaissance.

    a. <u>Life.</u> The following were important events of the life of Vittorino:

       (1) <u>Birth.</u> Vittorino was born *in Feltre, Italy, in 1378.* This small town was close to the city of Padua, which had a large university.

       (2) <u>Education.</u> He entered *the University of Padua* at eighteen and remained there for twenty years, first as a student and then as a teacher.

       (3) <u>First Humanist School.</u> In 1416 he began the first Humanist school. This school opened in *Venice.*

       (4) <u>Learns Greek.</u> Guarino, who had been a friend during the university days at Padua, taught Vittorino Greek.

       (5) <u>Padua and Venice.</u> In 1422 he accepted a professorship at Padua in Latin literature. Disturbed by the immorality of the students, he resigned after one year and returned to teaching in Venice. *His Venetian school became famous all over Europe.*

       (6) <u>Mantua.</u> He moved to Mantua later where he became *tutor to the children of the Marquis Gonzaga.* A special building was set aside on the estate which became known as *La Giocosa.*

       (7) <u>Teaching.</u> Vittorino continued teaching at La Giocosa for twenty-three years, until *he died in 1446.*

    b. <u>Features of his Educational Approach.</u> Vittorino used in his educational approach:

       (1) <u>Classical Pedigogical Principles.</u> The writings of *Plutarch, Cicero and, in particular, Quintilian* influenced Vittorino's educational aims and methods.

       (2) <u>Aim of Education.</u> The major goal of education should be the *development of good character.* The secondary purpose should be the cultivation of learning.

       (3) <u>Method.</u> Vittorino believed in *individual differences.* Each student proceeded at his own pace. Students who found difficulties in their studies were never punished. Rather, Vittorino encouraged his students by word and *aroused their interests by teaching through games.* It was his conviction that pleasant and comfortable surroundings contributed to pupil learning.

       (4) <u>Discipline.</u> Vittorino *did not believe in punishing* his students. He succeeded

in winning their *friendship* and controlled them through *love*. However, moral weaknesses were handled with greater sternness.

2. **GUARINO OF VERONA.** Guarino was a personal friend of Vittorino. He was educated at Padua and became *the outstanding scholar of Greek language and literature in the West.* His school was modeled after the typical humanist school of the time. This school became as famous in time as the school of Vittorino in Venice.

3. **DESIDERIUS ERASMUS.** Erasmus was *the last of the great humanist scholars.* He is important because:

   a. **Feared Ignorance.** He stressed *the importance of education.* Holding a view similar to Socrates of old, Erasmus believed that ignorance is the source of individual and social evil.
   b. **A Reformer.** Erasmus attempted to have the abuses within the Christian Church corrected. He wrote against superstition, ignorance and immorality. The religious abuses ought to be *corrected from within.* On this basis Erasmus opposed Luther.
   c. **Not a Classics Admirer.** Erasmus did not share the humanists' enthusiasm for classical literature. However, he was responsible for bringing humanism to England, through the *University of Oxford.*
   d. **Purposes of Education.** His purposes of education were (in the order of importance):

      (1) **Development of Piety**
      (2) **Love of Learning Through the Liberal Arts**
      (3) **Vocational Preparation**
      (4) **Good Manners.**

   e. **Method.** The educational method recommended by Erasmus was:

      (1) **Learning Languages.** Learn a language *by using that language.*
      (2) **Student Personality.** *Individual differences are important* in determining the kind of education a student should have.
      (3) **Discipline.** All physical punishment should be *abolished.*
      (4) **Technique.** Teach by games and stories to encourage interest.

   f. **Social Goals.** The family, the state and the Church should have a stake in the education of the child.
   g. **Works.** He was author of the following works, which have educational importance:

      (1) **Praise of Folly**
      (2) **The Education of a Christian Man**
      (3) **On the Liberal Education of Boys from the Beginning**
      (4) **On the Right Method of Instruction.**

4. **THE BRETHREN OF THE COMMON LIFE.** This religious order was founded in the late fourteenth century at Deventer in Holland. Its purpose was to help impoverished people through almsgiving and education. The schools of The Brethren,

widespread throughout northern Europe, gave an elementary education to the children of the poor. The order educated *Erasmus*, an illegitimate orphan who later joined their ranks. His importance has been dealt with above. *St. Thomas a Kempis and Nicholas of Cusa* were among the order's most important members. *Martin Luther* received his *early education* in one of the many German schools of The Brethren *at Magdeburg*.

HUMANISM

BEGINNINGS. The social and economic conditions of the Renaissance led to *enormous changes* in the social, religious and intellectual *life of Western Europe*. This period is called *the first modern period. The humanistic philosophy* that challenged the theocentricity of medieval times *endures* as an influential background of thought in the contemporary world.

THE MEANING OF HUMANISM. Humanism is a philosophical frame of reference which *elevates man* to a position of primary concern. *Any system of thought which looks to man's happiness and welfare upon earth as it's central concern is humanistic.*

RENAISSANCE HUMANISM. The humanism of the Renaissance is of *two types:*

1. **OLD HUMANISM.** This humanism began in Italy. It had the following characteristics:

   a. **Individualistic.** This type of humanistic thinking stressed the development of an aesthetic, creative *independent individual* capable of living a full, rich life.
   b. **Education.** The early humanistic movement stressed the type of *aristocratic education* available for the nobility and the wealthy. This education was characterized by:

      (1) **Curriculum.** The humanities replaced theology in the curriculum. The emphasis was upon the pleasure of living.
      (2) **Teaching Method.** The teacher stressed self-expression in the pupils. The dialectic by which pupils expounded orally the argument of a theological thesis gave way to the written theme. Interest and motivation were important elements in the classroom.

2. **NEW HUMANISM.** This type of humanism grew out of Italian humanism when humanistic thought moved into *northern Europe*. It possessed the following characteristics:

   a. **Socialistic.** This type of humanistic thinking stressed the *social improvement of humanity. Moral and social education* were more important than the goals of the individual in education.
   b. **Universal Education.** The later humanistic movement aimed at the universal education. This trend was the beginning of *free education for all*. It was characterized by:

      (1) **Curriculum.** Both Classical and Biblical literature were taught to provide literary and religious education *to improve society*.
      (2) **Teaching Method.** Many northern schools retained the teaching improvements

introduced earlier in Italy. Thus, the discipline was less harsh and provision was made for individual interest and ability. However, the methodology was subordinate to the *social aims of education.*

THE INFLUENCE OF HUMANISM. Humanism during the Renaissance was *a reaction* against the severe restrictions upon knowledge imposed by a theocentric society. With the revival of the pagan classics and the growth of wealth, the Renaissance man looked to *the present* for his happiness and welfare. Humanism influenced subseqent thinkers. Among these are:

1. **THE UTILITARIANS.** The philosophers Bentham and Mill stressed *social welfare* in their philosophies. *Human happiness exists when the great majority of humanity is happy.*
2. **NATURALISM.** Humanism led to the development of Naturalism. Naturalism repudiated all theological explanations for man and the universe. The only level of reality is the events which take place within nature. All of human experience can be *understood in terms of the ordinary activities of nature:*
3. **EDUCATIONAL INFLUENCE.** Humanism through naturalism led to the following educational developments (through the works of *Rousseau, Basedow, Pestalozzi, Herbart and Froebel,* which are described in subsequent chapters):

   a. **Guidance.** *The teacher must guide* the learning of the child.
   b. **Individualized Learning.** The educational process must follow the order of nature. *Learning occurs through individual experience* and is based on the effort to satisfy needs perceived by the individual.
   c. **Universal Free Education.** *Society is improved* when every citizen receives an education which permits the development of his potentiality.

9 | EDUCATION DURING THE REFORMATION

INTRODUCTION. When in the year 1517 Martin Luther nailed his *Ninety-five Theses* to the door of Wittenberg Cathedral, he set in motion the religious revolution that resulted in a century of war, Europe divided in religion, and a reformation among both Protestant and Catholic Christians. The resulting turmoil benefited education immeasurably.

BACKGROUND FACTORS OF THE PROTESTANT REFORMATION. The following are some of the factors which contributed to the Protestant Reformation:

1. **INDIVIDUALISM.** The spirit of individualism which was awakened during the Renaissance sought to defend *the rights of the individual* against the encroachments of institutions. The extension of this attitude to the individual's religious rights occurred during the Reformation period.
2. **SPIRIT OF CRITICISM.** The Catholic *criticism of religious abuses went unheeded by the Vatican.* During the Renaissance, secular and religious critics found fault with traditional Catholic doctrine, ritual, interpretation of the Scriptures, and conduct of the clergy.
3. **SECULARISM.** The growth of secular feeling during the Renaissance provided a fertile field for *the growth of hostile feelings toward religious institutions.*
4. **RELIGIOUS ABUSES.** The widespread immorality during the Renaissance in Italy affected the Church. *Religious leaders frequently led lives as corrupt as any in the secular world.* Luxury and sensuality invaded a Papacy very much in need of reform. Priests, entrusted with solicitation of funds for a new and more impressive St. Peter's Church, frequently abused the doctrine of religious indulgences, selling those indulgences for money.
5. **RISE OF SECULAR POLITICAL POWER.** The *most important single factor in the success of the Protestant revolution* was the assistance it received from secular political authority. The Princes of Germany and the Monarchy of England benefitted from a limitation of Papal power. Monasteries that were tax free owned rich lands which employed hundreds of farmers. Large sums of money, exacted from the countries of Europe, went to the enrichment of the Papal court. The seizing of church lands and the cutting of revenue which could be sent to the Vatican operated to check Vatican power and to increase the wealth and authority of the rulers of western European countries, particularly those of Germany and of England.
6. **POPULAR UNREST.** While many princes and aristocrats were affluent during the sixteenth century, the common man suffered economically. The impoverished commoner seemed *doomed to a life of periodic unemployment, inferior education and heavy taxation.* Church taxes and Church abuses provided many common people with attitudes receptive to Protestant doctrine.
7. **THE PRINTING PRESS.** With the invention of movable type in 1450 and the refinement of paper, *Protestant doctrine could be spread with great rapidity.* Henry VIII was able to demand the use of the same textbooks in every school in England.

Thanks to the printing press, the translation of the Bible by Luther could be distributed throughout Germany. Since this translation was in the vernacular, large numbers of people could read it with understanding.

CHARACTERISTICS OF THE NEWLY-ESTABLISHED PROTESTANT POWERS.

1. <u>**AUTHORITY OF THE BIBLE.**</u> In repudiating the authority of the Pope and of tradition, the Protestant reformers stressed *the unique place of Scripture in the guidance of human life.* It was necessary for every man to read the scriptures. If a man had faith, he received the gift of inspiration from the Holy Spirit to enable him to interpret the meaning of the Scriptures.

2. <u>**AUTHORITY OF THE CROWN.**</u> The secular state was accorded a place of pre-eminence in temporal affairs as well as in many ecclesiastical affairs. Luther taught that the Prince must protect the Church and correct it whenever it moved away from the precepts of the Bible. Calvin taught that a crime against the state was also a crime against God. Man must obey the state as he obeys God. In England the monarch became the head of the Church. This *tendency toward authoritarian state government* in place of religious authoritarianism, accounts for the widespread support of Protestant revolutionists by many temporal authorities.

3. <u>**FANATICISM.**</u> It is paradoxical that a movement which taught the sacredness of the individual's religious judgment and the responsibility of each man for his own salvation, resulted in such *persecution of those dissenting from the reformer's viewpoint.* In rejecting the dogmatism and infallibility of Rome, the reformers uniformly adopted these same characteristics for themselves. Through fanaticism, Protestant turned on Catholic and differing Protestants alike.

4. <u>**OPPOSES USE OF REASON.**</u> Reason was called a poisonous beast by Luther. All the Protestant revolutionists denigrated human reason. It was believed that Original Sin had so destroyed human nature that human reason was completely untrustworthy. Man must *depend entirely upon faith.* Through faith, man is able to receive the saving graces of God.

5. <u>**UNIVERSAL EDUCATION.**</u> England did not change its educational system. However, Germany led the way in organizing a state educational system which provided *free compulsory elementary education for every boy and girl.*

GERMAN PROTESTANTISM

INTRODUCTION. The following are important figures in German Protestant education:

1. <u>**MARTIN LUTHER**</u> (1483-1546). Luther, besides being a religious leader, was also important for his theory of education. This theory was implemented by *Melanchthon* in central and southern Germany, and *Bugenhagen* in northern Germany and Denmark. The following summarizes *Luther's* educational contributions:
   a. <u>Universal Education.</u> Luther believed that *every boy and girl* should receive *a free elementary education.* Since the Bible was the vehicle by which the individual man achieved the guidance necessary for salvation, it was imperative for each person to have the skill to read the Bible.
   b. <u>State Control of Education.</u> Luther placed the ultimate responsibility for education on the state. The state should have concern about education because the educational system would mold the individual who would defend and support the government. Because of the position of the state in education, Luther held that among its obligations were:

(1) **Financial Support.** The state should provide the financial support of every school.

(2) **Compulsory Attendance.** It should ensure the attendance of every child by passing *compulsory education laws.*

(3) **Supervision.** The state should *supervise* the curriculum, books, and teaching in the schools.

c. **Vocational Education.** Luther thought public instruction should occupy only a part of the school day. The remainder of the time should be employed by the pupils at home. *At home each child should receive training for an occupation in life through a period of apprenticeship.*

d. **Higher Education.** Luther believed that only those young men who demonstrated intellectual ability ought to be given the opportunity to attend a university. *He did not approve of higher education for women.* A woman's place was in the home. The purpose of women was to bear as many children as possible. *The purpose of higher education was to train men for either public or religious service.*

e. **Writings.** Luther's important writings that affect education were:

(1) *Letter to the Mayors and Aldermen of All Cities of Germany in Behalf of Christian Schools.*

(2) *Sermon on the Duty of Sending Children to School.*

2. **PHILIPP MELANCHTHON** (1497-1560). Melanchthon was *one of the most important figures in education* in Germany during the Reformation period. A life-long friend of Luther (after his death, his body was laid to rest alongside Luther in the University of Wittenburg), *Melanchthon shares with John Sturm the honor of being founders of the Gymnasium or secondary school of Germany.* These points sketch *Melanchthon's role in education:*

a. **Textbooks in Humanities.** Melanchthon received his Master's Degree at the age of seventeen. Realizing the inadequacy of the textbooks then in use, *he wrote a Greek grammar* when he was sixteen. This book went through forty-three editions over the next hundred years. Later, he wrote *a Latin grammar,* destined to be in use for over two hundred years. During his lifetime, Melanchthon *published 709 works,* exclusive of his letters. Among these diversified publishings are works in *psychology, religion, history, ethics, physics, rhetoric, and logic.*

b. **Book of Visitation.** It was necessary to provide the people with Bibles, other books and the knowledge of how to read them in order to carry out Luther's teaching. The task of eliminating illiteracy through the establishment of schools was entrusted to Melanchthon. *In 1527 he wrote the Book of Visitation, the first school survey* ever written. He recommended the following grouping of three-level organization school classes:

(1) **First Level.** The first level should study *German, basic Latin, reading, and writing. Religion* and morality should hold an important place in the teaching. Each reading should have some moral lesson for the young pupil. This level of education developed into the *Volksschule* or modern German elementary school. Although Melanchthon made no recommendation about the number of years to be spent at this or subsequent levels, six years came to be allotted to each level in the centuries to come.

(2) **Second Level.** The second level should be the *Latin grammar* school. This level became the *modern Gymnasium* of German education. *Grammar,*

dialectics and rhetoric in both Greek and Latin should be studied. Melanch-thon recommended this curriculum *to protect and defend the new faith*. In keeping with the thought of all humanists of his day, Melanchthon claimed that *classical studies* provided the means by which the student could assimi-late the *ideas inherent in the Greek and Latin writings*.

(3) Third Level. The third level was recommended for *the university student* preparing to serve the Church and the State in the professions of religion, law, medicine or teaching.

c. Status of Teachers. Melanchthon held teaching in the highest regard. A teacher was viewed as *the protector of truth and justice* in the land. He served both Church and State. Although teachers were paid very little in Reformation Ger-many (most university professors worked for wages less than that paid to a bartender), the status of teachers became higher. The prestige enjoyed by Euro-pean teachers in subsequent ages is due largely to the efforts of Melanchthon.

d. Founder of Schools. While Melanchthon actively defended Lutheranism in the controversies among German theologians (he wrote the *Augsburg Confession* in 1530), his work in education went on until his death. The Volksschule, Gym-nasium and several universities came into being through his efforts. A year before his death in 1560, the *first state system of education* made its appearance in the *Duchy of Wurttemberg*. A century after this event, all of Germany was organized in this pattern of education.

3. JOHANNES BUGENHAGEN. Bugenhagen was entrusted with the establishment of Lutheran schools in northern Germany. His success in building elementary schools throughout the area brought him to the attention of the King of Denmark. He re-ceived a commission to organize Lutheran elementary schools in Denmark. Some historians have credited him with being the father of the Volksschule. His great *success in establishing these schools in Denmark* and in northern Germany led to this admiration among educational historians.

4. JOHANNES STURM. *Sturm established a school for boys* between the ages of seven and seventeen *at Strasbourg in 1537*. This school relied heavily upon a Latin cur-riculum. Sturm called his school the "Gymnasium." Although this humanistic school did not remain on the educational scene for long, *the name and organization* of the school was adopted by subsequent German secondary schools.

PROTESTANT REVOLT IN SWITZERLAND. The major Protestant reformers important to education were:

1. HULDREICH ZWINGLI (1484-1531). Zwingli was the first to introduce Protestant-ism into Switzerland. Some important contributions of Zwingli were:

a. Before Luther. Zwingli began *preaching against the superstitions and evils of the Roman Church* prior to the publication of the ninety-five theses of Luther. Three visits to Italy as an army chaplain revealed the nature of the Papacy to him.

b. Upheld in Zurich. Pope Adrian VI asked the people of Zurich to repudiate Zwingli after the latter had published an *attack upon the law of celibacy* for clerics. The town council upheld Zwingli and declared the town independent from the Bishop of Constance.

c. Published Declaration. In 1522 Zwingli published the *Architeles* which was a *declaration of spiritual freedom* from the hierarchy.

d. **Reforms Spread.** The reforms of Zwingli spread to all but the forest Cantons of Switzerland. He taught that *the congregation of people,* not the hierarchy, constituted the Church.

e. **Important Doctrines.** Some of his more important teachings were:

   (1) **Scripture.** Scripture is the sole rule of faith.

   (2) **Freedom of Conscience.** Freedom of conscience for each individual Christian is necessary.

   (3) **Individual Interpretation.** Each individual must interpret the Scriptures for himself, under the guidance of the Holy Spirit.

   (4) **No Idols.** Worship of holy pictures and statues is evil.

   (5) **The Mass.** The Mass has no support in Scripture.

   (6) **Purgatory.** Neither has the existence of Purgatory any support in Scripture.

   (7) **God and Man.** Christ is the only mediator necessary for man.

   (8) **Saints.** Prayer to saints is evil.

   (9) **Civil Authority.** Church affairs are subject to civil authority.

  (10) **Marriage.** Marriage is lawful and desirable for all mankind.

f. **Educational Contributions.** Some important educational activities of Zwingli were:

   (1) **An Influential Book.** He wrote the *Christian Education of Youth* in 1523. This was translated into Swiss and widely distributed.

   (2) **Universal Elementary Education.** Zwingli recommended universal elementary education in order *to enable every Christian to read the Scriptures.*

   (3) **Curriculum.** He suggested that the curriculum contain *classical, humanistic and religious subjects.*

   (4) **Reforms Carried Out.** His educational reforms were *put into practice by his successor, John Calvin.*

2. **JOHN CALVIN (1509-1569).** Calvin was one of the greatest figures in the Protestant Reformation. The following are *some important biographical details of Calvin:*

a. **Education.** Educated thoroughly in the humanist tradition, Calvin studied law. He *studied theology at the University of Paris.*

b. **Forced to Flee.** His support of the Protestant Reformation forced him to flee to *Basle,* Switzerland, in 1535.

c. **His Theological System.** He wrote a complete outline of his theological system in 1535, called *The Institutes of the Christian Religion.*

d. **Became Leader.** William Farel, who won the support of the Council of Geneva for the Reformation, invited Calvin *to lead the movement in Geneva.*

e. **Theocratic Dictatorship.** After a brief exile from Geneva in Strasbourg, Calvin returned to Geneva in 1542. He established a theocratic dictatorship there, *ruling as Chairman of the Council until his death in 1569.*

f. **Church and State.** He united Church and State to such an extent that moral offenses were punishable by the State. During the first twenty-two years of his rule, fifty-eight people were executed, fourteen witches were burned to death, hundreds were exiled and hundreds more were punished annually for moral offenses. All places of popular pleasure were closed. Dress regulations were severe. Prisoners were tortured to exact confessions of moral offenses.

g. **Important Doctrines.** Some of the doctrines Calvin preached were:

(1) **Depravity of Man.** Human nature is totally depraved because of the sin of Adam.

(2) **Supremacy of Scripture.** *Human reason* is so thoroughly *limited* by man's depravity and his insignificance in comparison to the holiness and immensity of God, that God provided the inspired Scriptures to teach man the truth.

(3) **Interpreters of Scripture.** The interpretations which he and his appointed ministers made of the Scriptures must be accepted. *Calvin claimed an infallibility* which he denied to the Popes and tradition.

(4) **Simplicity of Faith.** Calvin *repudiated the Mass and the veneration of Mary, the Saints, images and pictures.* He considered these actions idolatrous.

(5) **Predestination.** Man can do nothing by himself to achieve the reward of *Heaven.* The act of faith in Christ, by which he lives a pious life of conformity to the Scriptures, indicates that he is predestined for *salvation.* God destines some human beings for an afterlife of eternal fire in *Hell.* He does this to demonstrate His infinite Justice. There is no middle state of Purgatory.

h. **Contributions to Education.** The education demanded by Calvin in Geneva *was adopted by the Massachusetts Bay Colony in colonial New England.* The Calvinist theocratic state of colonial New England influenced the development of American education in turn. The following are the recommendations of Calvin:

(1) **Universal Education.** There should be universal education for all boys and girls.

(2) **Compulsory Education.** Every child should have compulsory education *enforced by the state* during the elementary years.

(3) **State Support.** There should be state support of education. No tuition charges should be made of the children.

(4) **Secondary Schools.** Calvin established the *"colleges"* which were Latin secondary schools to teach a curriculum consisting of the trivium and classics.

(5) **University.** He founded the *"Academie,"* a university to train gifted boys for Church and State service.

i. **Importance of Calvin.** Although there are very few today who completely accept the theology of Calvin, his educational influence has been great. Perhaps the tolerance of high interest rates and the encouragement of modern business practices by the Geneva dictator won the allegiance of many German and Dutch middle class business interests. Calvinism spread into the Netherlands, parts of Germany, France, England and Scotland.

PROTESTANTISM IN ENGLAND

INTRODUCTION. Although Henry VIII declared the English Church free of Roman control in the *Act of Supremacy in 1534,* Protestantism did not officially replace Roman Catholicism until Edward VI came to the throne in 1547. Anglicanism became the official State religion with the passage of the *Acts of Supremacy and Uniformity in 1558,* during the reign of Elizabeth I. Unlike its Continental form, English Protestantism retained many Roman Catholic doctrines. They rejected Papal authority, retained the hierarchical and parish organization, and made the Church nationalistic in its subjection to the English Crown. As a result of this, *the educational system did not possess the universal characteristics* common in Germany. Education remained under *Church control.* Only in this case, the Church was the Anglican Protestant Church of England.

ENGLISH EDUCATION PRIOR TO THE REFORMATION. Education before the reign of Henry VIII could be summarized thus:

1. **CHURCH DOMINATION.** There were *very few secular schools in England before the Reformation.* The universities were controlled by the religious orders. *The Latin grammar schools were established by:*

   a. Monasteries
   b. Cathedrals
   c. Music or chantry schools attached to the cathedral
   d. Colleges
   e. Hospitals.

2. **AIM OF EDUCATION.** The purpose of education in general was *the production of spiritual citizens* in a Christian world.

3. **CURRICULUM OF LATIN GRAMMAR SCHOOL.** The Latin grammar school taught *the usual trivium and quadrivium.* In England the curricular emphasis was upon grammar. When Erasmus visited Oxford toward the turn of the sixteenth century, he awakened interest in the humanities and classical literature popular during the Renaissance. This Renaissance came to England *after the reformation.* As a result it affected the curriculum of the Latin grammar schools after the rise of Protestantism.

4. **GROWTH OF COLLEGES.** The English university was constituted of a group of semi-autonomous colleges. *The importance of the colleges was unique to English educational development.* There was no individualization of the curriculum. Each class studied the common curriculum proper for the year. Each college prescribed the rules for the academic and moral behavior of its students.

ENGLISH EDUCATION AFTER THE REFORMATION. After Protestantism became the established religion of England, these changes took place:

1. **NO ROMAN CATHOLIC SCHOOLS.** When Henry VIII closed the Catholic monasteries, the monastic schools were terminated. At the end of the reign of Edward VI, about *forty-one grammar schools remained* in all of England. Two hundred fifty-nine grammar schools had been dissolved. This affected the number of college graduates. In a fifty-year period *the number of graduates was reduced* by fifty percent.

2. **CHURCH DOMINATION.** During the reign of Elizabeth I, education was placed under the regulation of the Anglican Church. These regulations were:

   a. **Visitation.** The Anglican Bishop was required *to visit every school in his district at least once during the year.* On this occasion, the bishop would inquire into the orthodoxy and behavior of the teacher. If a teacher were considered suspect, he was immediately removed from his position.
   b. **Clerical Teaching.** Members of *the Anglican clergy were required to teach.* One thirtieth of their salary had to be donated to needy young scholars.
   c. **Teacher Certification.** By 1581 every teacher in England *required a license granted by the Anglican Church.* By 1662 *an oath of conformity* to the State religion was demanded of every teacher as a prerequisite for a license.

3. **SOURCE OF NEW SCHOOLS.** Schools were established by the guilds, the Crown, a town council or endowment by an aristocrat.

4. **UNIFORMITY OF CURRICULUM AND TEXTBOOKS.** With the use of printing presses, the Protestant edition of the *Bible* was distributed to all schools. The *same textbooks* were required in every school of the Realm.

5. **CURRICULUM.** The trivium and the quadrivium of the former grammar schools continued in the schools of the Reformation. *Classical literature,* which had been widespread upon the Continent a century earlier, became part of the curriculum of the grammar schools at this time. The major emphasis of every *grammar school* concentrated upon *grammar and classical literature.* Some few grammar schools introduced *archery or drama or English history* as secondary activities.

6. **AIM OF EDUCATION.** The general purpose of education was *the production of patriotic Anglican Englishmen.*

7. **NO GOVERNMENT INTERFERENCE.** One of the most important characteristics of English education influential to the development of American education was *the absence of government regulation or support of the school system* after assigning it to the State Church.

8. **LATIN GRAMMAR SCHOOL.** The following describes *some characteristics of Latin grammar school education:*

   a. **High Drop Out Rate.** The majority of those pupils who entered the Latin grammar school dropped out before they finished. This was attributable to the *rigid standards* of the curriculum.

   b. **Pupil Ages.** Pupils usually began their education in the Latin grammar school at the age of *seven* and completed their education at *sixteen.* At this time the young student was ready for entrance to the university.

   c. **School Year.** The majority of ordinary Latin grammar schools conducted school *six days a week for forty-eight weeks.* Two vacation periods were permitted.

   d. **School Day.** The school day began in winter promptly at seven a.m. and continued until five p.m. Because of the added light in summertime, the day began one hour earlier and lasted one hour later in the evening. Here is a specimen timetable of a summer day:

      (1) <u>6–8 a.m.</u> Latin and Greek grammar were studied.
      (2) <u>8–9 a.m.</u> A study period.
      (3) <u>9–11 a.m.</u> Homework was recited, and extemporaneous translations into Latin or Greek were made.
      (4) <u>11 a.m.–1 p.m.</u> Lunch period. A Bible reading took place during lunch.
      (5) <u>1–3 p.m.</u> Classical literature was studied, followed by translations, parsing and memory work.
      (6) <u>3–4 p.m.</u> Recess.
      (7) <u>4–6 p.m.</u> After rhetoric came figures of speech in classical literature and Bible. Themes were then assigned for homework, to be presented the following day.

   e. **Grades.** Each pupil proceeded *at his own pace through six units or grades.* The pupil was expected to read and write Latin and Greek by the time he completed the sixth grade. The usual sixth grader wrote themes and poems in either of these classical languages.

   f. **Latin and Greek Dominance.** The Latin and Greek classical literature and grammar dominated the curriculum of the Latin grammar schools *until 1650.* By the middle of the seventeenth century, *Latin declined* throughout Europe as the language of scholarship.

g. **Discipline.** Punishment was *very severe* in most Latin grammar schools. Children received a flogging for violations of the rules of behavior. Frequently, failure in academics resulted in hitting the pupil with a ruler.

9. **PROMINENT EDUCATORS.** Two important educators of this period were *Roger Ascham and Richard Mulcaster.*

   a. **Ascham.** Roger Ascham is important for his treatise upon education entitled the *"Scholemaster."* He *disapproved of the flogging* of children which was common in the Latin grammar schools at this time. He felt that the teacher ought *to encourage the pupils.* The manner of the teacher ought to be cheerful. Excessive work in Latin and Greek grammar can discourage a good pupil. Ascham stressed the importance of *moral training.*
   b. **Mulcaster.** Richard Mulcaster taught at the Merchants'-Taylors' School and at St. Paul's School in London. He wrote two treatises on education. He suggested that the *educational method be based upon the child's nature.* Children are *ready* at different periods for further work. Mulcaster suggested that the good teacher encourage and reward the pupils with approval, taking care to prevent any idleness. He must stimulate the pupil's memory. A child *must never be beaten for his inability to learn.* Mulcaster hoped for *universal and free education.* He considered a man had not completed his elementary education until he could read and write with ease in the classical languages.

THE CATHOLIC REFORMATION

INTRODUCTION. The Council, called by Pope Paul III in 1555 at Trent, put into action the internal forces necessary for *a reform from within the Church.* In order to stem the tide of Protestant growth and achieve the necessary reform suggested by the Council's eighteen years of deliberation, the Catholic Church depended largely upon *an educated clergy and laity.* New regulations were made which governed the seminary training of priests. *New religious orders* carried out the education of the laity.

THE SOCIETY OF JESUS. No religious order approached the *Society of Jesus or Jesuits,* as they were called, in defending the faith of Roman Catholicism. The *school system* which they introduced into Europe was *one of the best educational systems ever conceived by man* up to this time. Many Protestants sent their children to Jesuit schools. The schools and universities of the Jesuit order *trained most of the world's great philosophers and writers* until modern times. Every *new advance* in educational methodology, teacher training, supervision and administration began with the *"Plan of Studies,"* first published by the Jesuit order in *1599.* This order was founded by *St. Ignatius of Loyola* and was accepted by the Pope in *1540.*

IGNATIUS OF LOYOLA. A biographical sketch of Ignatius should include:

1. **YOUTH.** Ignatius was *born in 1491* at Loyola in northern Spain. He received his early training at Court. As a young adult Ignatius was an officer in the Spanish army. Both of his legs were broken in battle in 1520. The ensuing convalescence afforded him the opportunity of reading the *Life of Christ and the Lives of the Saints.* These books led him to turn toward a religious life.
2. **RECLUSE.** In 1522 Ignatius lived as a religious hermit in a cave in the village of Manresa in Spain. During this period he wrote a handbook of spirituality called

Spiritual Exercises. He set out on a pilgrimage to Jerusalem in 1523. It was his intention to remain in Jerusalem in order to convert the Mohammedan world. However, he was sent back to Venice after spending six weeks in the Holy City.

3. <u>STUDENT.</u> In 1524, determined to serve the Church, he realized the necessity of obtaining a sound intellectual education. He *entered the Latin grammar school* at Barcelona, Spain. Ignatius walked to Paris to study at its university in 1528. He received a Master's Degree in 1534.

4. <u>THE JESUITS.</u> Beginning with three friends from the University of Paris, Ignatius founded the religious order which became *the Society of Jesus* when the Pope accepted the order in 1540. The Jesuit Order was organized along *military lines.* It demanded vows of *poverty, chastity and absolute obedience.* Ignatius was elected the *first General* and he occupied this position until his *death in 1556.* This religious order has thousands of members today, with schools and colleges or universities *all over the world.*

RATIO STUDIORUM. A committee of Jesuit scholars and teachers *worked for fifteen years to produce a plan for education.* In 1599 the plan was put into practice. It proved to be the best system ever devised in education up to the sixteenth century. *Voltaire,* who studied with the Jesuits, claimed that the best years of his life were spent in Jesuit schools. The following represents the *educational principles contained in the "Plan of Studies":*

1. <u>AIM OF EDUCATION.</u> The purpose of education is to prepare man for effective living in this world and eternal happiness with God in eternity. The graduate of a Jesuit school was expected *to think clearly and logically, to express himself* effectively, eloquently and persuasively both *in speech and in writing, to love learning and to possess erudition.*

2. <u>TEACHER TRAINING.</u> For the first time in history a deliberate effort was made *to select, train and supervise* the very best teachers. Teacher training consisted of:

   a. <u>Personal Inclination.</u> No one was forced into teaching for any reason. Those students who exhibited *a desire to teach* had the first prerequisite for teaching.

   b. <u>University Graduate.</u> Prior to entering the academy of teaching, a student was required to *demonstrate his success in academic work.*

   c. <u>Selection for the Teacher Academy.</u> Only those students who received *grades with distinction in the oral examinations* during their academic careers would be considered. These examinations tested the student's ability to explain clearly, to defend logically and to persuade effectively.

   d. <u>Teacher Observation.</u> During the final year of study at the academy of teaching, the student was required *to observe the teaching of a master teacher.* He would confer with this teacher about the methods used and the purposes of his teaching.

   e. <u>Practice Teaching.</u> The student was required to demonstrate satisfactory ability in teaching. *Three times a week* he met with the Prefect of Studies in order to *give demonstration lessons.* The Prefect corrected the methods of the student teacher.

   f. <u>Trial Teaching.</u> After the student graduated, *he received careful supervision* as a beginner teacher. Twice a month the Prefect of Studies visited his classroom to correct or praise his teaching. After two years, the Prefect paid the teacher routine visits once a month.

3. **THE JESUIT TEACHER.** The teacher in the grammar schools remained with the same class, year after year. This enabled him *to know* thoroughly the *capacities and personalities* of his pupils. The following expectations were required of the teacher:

a. **Enthusiasm.** The teacher *had to be enthusiastic* about teaching. If he were lacking in this motivation, it was assumed that he would be ineffective. When the teacher became tired after a few years of teaching, he was given time off for personal study and a temporary change of duties.

b. **Just.** The teacher could show *no favoritism* in his class. He had to be fair with every student.

c. **Know Each Student.** The Jesuit teacher was expected to know as much as possible about each student. The interests, temperaments, abilities, attitudes and capacities of every student were carefully studied during the years he remained with the same class.

d. **Guidance and Tutoring.** After the classes were finished, the teacher remained at his desk. He was available therefore for any *personal guidance* required by his students. If a student found his lessons difficult, he had the opportunity to obtain *additional clarification and instruction* from his teacher.

e. **Interest in Youth.** Although every Jesuit teacher was expected to be *educated and intelligent*, he also had to possess a *sincere interest* in the youths being educated.

f. **Creative Teaching.** The teacher was required to be obedient in important matters. His vow demanded immediate obedience of all orders. The teacher was *not at liberty to change the curriculum* to suit his own interests or to introduce ideas contrary to Catholic doctrine. However, he was expected to be *creative in classroom methodology*.

g. **Individualized Instruction.** The Jesuit teacher was expected to enhance group instruction by providing *individual teaching* for each pupil at the teacher's desk while the class was engaged in composition work or some similar activity.

4. **THE CURRICULUM.** The curriculum of the grammar school gave heavy emphasis to *Latin grammar, the humanities and rhetoric*. The curriculum of Jesuit schools changed in succeeding centuries as the needs and social conditions changed. *In 1832 and in 1906* the *Ratio* was changed in curriculum matters in order to modernize Jesuit lower and higher education. The Jesuit curriculum was *the first to provide educational continuity* from grade one through graduation.

5. **THE SCHOOL DAY.** The children in the Jesuit schools were not burdened as heavily as the pupils of the English grammar school. Pupils spent *two and a half hours* in class in the *morning* and *two hours* in class during the *afternoon*. The remainder of the afternoon was spent in *games and athletic sports*. The pupils were allowed *one school holiday* each week.

6. **METHODOLOGY.** The teacher employed *a variety of the following methods:*
a. **Prelection.** The teacher would *read a passage, return to explain it* line by line, discuss with the class each point and add cultural information where applicable.

b. **The Three Rs.** The teacher must constantly *repeat, review and reward*.

c. **Concertatio.** This was an *open class discussion*, identical with the developmental method of teaching employed in many social studies classrooms today.

d. **Dialogue and Debate.** *At times the teacher might engage in a dialogue with a student* to dramatically bring forth intellectual conflicts. *Debates between* *students* over strongly felt issues, following the laws of logic, were encouraged at times.

e. Student Reports and Speeches. Students were encouraged to give *oral reports upon topics of interest.* Each pupil would be provided with the opportunity to deliver a speech *imitating the style* of famous speakers.

f. Imitation in Writing and Speaking. The student *learned a style of writing or speaking by imitation* of the experts in the field.

g. Group Competition. The classroom was considered divided into two battalions, armed with ideas and in a state of constant war. One group *competed against the other in readiness to correct or to inform* the intellectual lapses of the other.

7. **DISCIPLINE AND PROMOTION.** The teacher *never punished* any pupil. He was expected *to be a teacher and not a disciplinarian.* In the event of *a serious* disciplinary problem the pupil was sent to a school official called a *Corrector.* The Corrector was never a member of the Jesuit order. If the student persisted in his bad behavior, he was dismissed from the school. Those pupils who *demonstrated their lack of aptitude for scholarship* were dismissed from the school. The grammar school had *five grades.* A pupil remained about *two years in each grade.* Although pupils were usually promoted each year, *gifted students* could be *promoted anytime.* Pupils unable to do advanced work were held back. At times some pupils might be demoted if it became apparent that they were unable to do the work of a higher grade.

8. **REWARDS.** Students who did well were constantly rewarded by *the commendation of the teacher.* The outstanding scholars in each area were *awarded medals* at a formal exercise before the entire school. This practice continues in Jesuit schools today with the commencement awards in scholarship for each area of the curriculum. It was believed that rewards offered incentive and encouragement for continued efforts and success in studies. The outstanding students in composition in each class were named *class officers.* The teacher appointed one *decurion* for every ten pupils. The decurion was rewarded for his personal responsibility and integrity as well as his academic success in the class. It was the duty of the decurion to hear homework recitations or to collect homework papers among his ten pupils, keeping a detailed record for each pupil.

9. **SCHOOL ADMINISTRATION.** The administration of the Jesuit grammar school was divided into:

a. Prefect of Studies. The Prefect of Studies was responsible for the *administration of the school.* His duties required the *supervision of all of his teachers* at least once every month. This classroom visit inspected the teacher's methodology, schedule, teaching content and improvement.

b. Assistant to the Prefect. The Prefect was provided with an Assistant *to help with the administrative chores.*

c. The Corrector. The Corrector was always an outsider, selected for his ability in understanding the young and carrying out effective *disciplinary measures* in serious cases.

d. The Faculty. In addition to teaching responsibilities, the faculty were required to meet together twice a month in order *to exchange ideas* and to receive any information the Prefect desired to communicate.

IMPORTANCE OF JESUIT EDUCATION. It remains *a vital force in education today* with schools and universities throughout the free world. Jesuit education is important because it was the first educational system to demand these innovations:

1. <u>**TRAINING OF TEACHERS.**</u> *Systematic training* for future teachers was a necessity.
2. **SUPERVISION.** *Organized supervision of every teacher* came into operation.
3. <u>**TEACHER EDUCATION.**</u> The Jesuit educational system *required selection procedures* for teacher education.
4. <u>**NEW TEACHERS.**</u> *Practice teaching and careful supervision* during the initial years of a teaching career were stressed.
5. <u>**METHODOLOGY.**</u> A high premium was placed on *methodology in teaching.*
6. <u>**TRAINING.**</u> The training was based upon *sound principles of human behavior.*
7. <u>**GRADUATES.**</u> *Excellence in all teacher graduates* was regarded as standard procedure.

10 | EDUCATION DURING THE AGE OF REASON

INTRODUCTION. The seventeenth century has been called *the beginning of modern times*. It was an age of scientific inquiry and a time of philosophical rationalism. The following *characteristics of the seventeenth century* are given as a background to the time:

1. **POLITICAL TURMOIL.** The early years of the seventeenth century were characterized by *religious warfare, civil strife and scientific growth*. The Thirty Years War devastated Germany and Central Europe. In England the struggle between Parliament and the Stuarts ended with the *execution of Charles II*. In science the *Copernican theory and Galileo's experiments* began scientific progress utilizing a new method and rejected ancient authority. Observation, facts, reason and truth were stressed in ways different from medieval thought.

2. **RATIONALISM.** Great reliance was placed upon the use of reason. Acceptance of the universality of reason led to optimism about the progress of human life. It led also to a lack of interest in emotion. Once political stability was achieved during the final years of this century, the values held high were those highlighting *restraint, order and reason*. Reason was applied to every area of human life, including religion, government and society. The rational criticism put into motion with the Cartesian "doubt" led to deism, democracy and individualism in subsequent centuries. This overemphasis of reason resulted in a new emphasis upon emotion during the romanticism of a future century.

FRANCIS BACON. Francis Bacon is typical of this age. As a philosopher he *stressed the empirical method* of science for arriving at reliable knowledge. The emphasis he placed upon *observation and experimentation* gave induction a higher role in the reasoning processes than deduction, which ruled human thinking from classical times on. He is most famous for his *"idols"* or those *tendencies which lead man's mind astray of the truth*. These idols illustrate the *undesirability of placing complete reliance upon assumptions and principles which have not been verified* by observation and experimentation. Subsequent philosophers found it necessary to meet this problem in the presentation of their system of thought. The following is a list of Bacon's "idols:"

1. **IDOLS OF THE TRIBE.** These tendencies toward intellectual error derive from *the nature of humanity* in general:

   a. **Common Sense.** The tendency to rely upon *limited assumptions* without verifying them as established truths.
   b. **Beliefs.** Man has a tendency to support his *personal beliefs*.
   c. **Wishful Thinking.** Wishful thinking is the tendency to believe *what one wishes to believe*.
   d. **Overgeneralization.** The tendency to *jump to conclusions* on the basis of first

impressions.

    e. **Ultimate Causes.** The tendency to *describe the cause* of a thing without verifying this assumed cause.

2. **IDOLS OF THE CAVE.** These tendencies toward intellectual error derive from the *nature of the individual man.*

    a. **Insularity.** The tendency to overemphasize *the area of knowledge* or the subject with which one is familiar.

    b. **Conservatism.** The tendency to admire and *prefer the past.*

    c. **Novelty.** The opposite of Conservatism is Novelty, the tendency to admire and *prefer anything new.*

    d. **Authority.** Authority is often based on the tendency to accept authoritative propositions *without critically evaluating* the proposition.

    e. **Inertia.** The tendency to *bypass intellectually difficult problems.*

3. **IDOLS OF THE MARKET PLACE.** These tendencies towards intellectual error derive from the act of *human communication.*

    a. **Meaningless Words.** The tendency to *create* words which are *so general* that they become meaningless to others.

    b. **Double-Meaning Words.** The tendency *not to clarify* the specific meaning in which a word is employed.

    c. **Personal Definitions.** The tendency to employ words whose *meanings are entirely personal.*

    d. **Verbalisms.** The tendency *to attribute significance* to insignificant words or phrases.

    e. **Jargon.** The tendency *to accept large words* which transcend one's understanding.

4. **IDOLS OF THE THEATER.** These tendencies towards intellectual error derive from *the things one has learned in the past.*

    a. **Experimentation.** The tendency which derives from the *dogmatism and rigidity in one's learning* that leads toward the acceptance of propositions that are not verifiable by the senses.

    b. **Superstition.** The tendency to interpret all of *reality in terms of religious authoritative beliefs.*

EDUCATIONAL IMPORTANCE. Bacon is important to education because:

1. **SCIENTIFIC INQUIRY.** He stressed the importance of *relying upon the method of science* for establishing principles of action, rather than upon an undue reverence for the writings of the past. Today the social science of education proposes principles of education upon the basis of the experimental methods alone. While the educationist reveres the memory of the great thinkers of the past and accepts many of their statements as hypotheses for future investigation, he is *not chained to any one favored theory.*

2. **AWARE OF ERROR.** The idols demonstrate the ease with which one may reason fallaciously. Teachers today are aware of these tendencies. As a result they develop the thinking skills of their students.

MICHEL DE MONTAIGNE. Although Montaigne lived during the latter years of the sixteenth century, his writings were more appropriate for the century to come.

EDUCATIONAL IMPORTANCE. Montaigne wrote on education in his "Essays:"

1. AIM OF EDUCATION. The real life of a man is lived in his thoughts. The purpose of education ought to be the development of his *ability to formulate judgments.* A man must depend upon his *reason* in arriving at truth. Education should provide him with the opportunity of judging things for himself.
2. METHOD OF EDUCATION. Montaigne believed that teaching should take place in an *atmosphere of freedom and kindness.* He would abolish any physical punishment. Fear serves only to enhance the behavioral characteristics it is designed to halt, once the individual is free.

RENE DESCARTES and JAN AMOS COMENIUS

DESCARTES. (1596-1650). Rene Descartes was a mediocre scientist, a great mathematician and an even greater philosopher. He is considered to be *the father of modern philosophy.* His thought *affected educational theory* in the following manner:

1. EDUCATION A NATURAL RIGHT OF MAN. Since knowledge is attained through the reasoning processes, every man has *the right to develop the innate faculties of his soul.* Although men learn at different paces, education is possible for all.
2. IMPORTANCE OF DOUBTING AUTHORITATIVE PROPOSITIONS. It is necessary for man to doubt everything prior to asserting any definite truths. *This act of doubt leads the mind to the rational assertion* of a self-evident principle that cannot be doubted. Therefore, it is possible to infer the right of each man to think for himself.
3. CLEAR AND CERTAIN TRUTHS. Man ought to accept no statement as true, unless it appears clear and certain to his intellect.
4. PSYCHOLOGICAL PRINCIPLES OF KNOWLEDGE. In the act of knowing, the mind proceeds from what is already known to the unknown. This infers *the need for a teacher* to base learning upon the intellectual experience of each pupil. Descartes asserted the principle that the mind moves from *the concrete to the abstract, the simple to the more complex.* These principles underlie the organization of school curriculum.

JAN AMOS COMENIUS

INFLUENCES UPON COMENIUS. The two major influences upon the educational thought of Comenius were Francis Bacon (see earlier chapter), and Wolfgang Ratke.

WOLFGANG RATKE. (1571-1635). Ratke was a Lutheran schoolmaster who won the support of Prince Ludwig of Anhalt Kothen in establishing a school along the lines of a new methodology. Although the school failed after one year, Ratke's ideas were influential upon the thought of that great educational figure, Comenius. These theories of Ratke were contained in his work, "The New Method," which was published in 1617. Some of these principles of education were:

1. EXPERIENCE. Learning must proceed from experience. The child was expected *to observe and to use* whatever was taught. He would not rely upon words alone.
2. OPPOSED LEARNING BY ROTE. Ratke believed that *memorization by rote of*

Latin and Greek grammar was both harmful and useless. He relegated Latin to the fourth grade and Greek to the sixth grade. He did not require any memorization by rote. Ratke held class discussions to insure understanding of the material.

3. <u>SELF-DISCIPLINE.</u> Rules were not to be imposed upon the children. They were *expected to set their own regulations* and to abide by them *without adult interference.*

LIFE OF COMENIUS. Comenius was a kind and gentle Moravian Bishop who lived in an age of violence that brought heartbreak to him. An account of his life, divided into four sections, follows:

1. <u>EARLY YEARS.</u> Comenius was *born 1592 in Nivnice, Czechoslovakia.* His family were Moravians, a religious sect that took its name from the Province of Moravia and followed the teachings of the matyred John Huss. This group desired only to lead quiet simple lives, piously following the Scriptures. Consequently, they were persecuted by Catholic and Protestant alike.

2. <u>SCHOOLING.</u> Comenius attended *school in the village of Nivnice.* He described this experience in painful terms. The school demanded learning by rote of Latin grammar. The teacher drove home his lesson with physical punishment. Comenius completed his *theological studies at the University of Heidelberg.*

3. <u>TEACHER AND MINISTER.</u> Comenius returned to the province of Moravia in 1614. Because of his youth, he could not be ordained for two years. During this time, Comenius *taught school* and began his lifelong work in education. After his *ordination,* he was assigned as pastor and superintendent of schools in a Moravian village. *Spanish troops looted and burned this village in 1621, during the Thirty Years War.* Comenius lost his manuscripts as well as all his possessions when his home was burnt to the ground. He barely escaped. However, he moved to Poland where he became the *headmaster of a Gymnasium in the city of Lissa.* In 1625 Comenius was elected a bishop in the Moravian Church. His writings in education, originally intended for his own school, became known throughout Europe. They were received enthusiastically everywhere.

4. <u>WRITER.</u> Comenius moved to England in the hope of gaining support for the writing of a universal encyclopedia. Failing to achieve the necessary backing, *he moved to Sweden* where he was supported in the writing of textbooks for Swedish schools by a Dutch nobleman. After five years, Comenius was elected *Senior Bishop of the Moravian Church* and he returned to Lissa, Poland. Between 1650 and 1654, Comenius ran a school in Hungary. After he again returned to Poland, he supported the Swedish effort to conquer Poland. *In 1657* the Polish people turned against the Moravians because of the support the Moravians gave the Protestant army, and they *destroyed the city of Lissa.* Comenius lost everything he had, including his manuscripts of the Czech language grammar, sermons and encyclopedia. He moved to Amsterdam, Holland. In Amsterdam Comenius brought out another edition of *"The Great Didactic." He died in 1670,* a broken man.

EDUCATIONAL CONTRIBUTIONS OF COMENIUS. Some important contributions Comenius made to education were:

1. <u>PRE-SCHOOL TRAINING.</u> He anticipated Pestalozzi and Freobel in recommending *sense training* for the pre-school child.

2. <u>CURRICULUM.</u> Comenius proposed a *curriculum for primary elementary education* that is used in the primary grades today.

3. <u>**SUBJECTS RECOMMENDED.**</u> He recommended the study of *science and social studies* in the secondary school.

4. <u>**METHOD.**</u> He emphasized the fact that *learning comes through the senses*. The teacher must adapt his methods to this principle. Whenever possible the teacher must *be concrete*, permit the child *to observe* for himself, and arrange for the child to have *direct experience in learning by doing*.

5. <u>**THE SCHOOL.**</u> Comenius suggested that the *school experience be made as pleasant as possible*. He proposed that the school year be limited to forty-two weeks, that the teacher make use of play in teaching children, and that the school surroundings be made as attractive as possible.

6. <u>**AN OLD BELIEF.**</u> He reaffirmed Quintilian's belief in the need for *personal motivation* in learning.

7. <u>**DISCIPLINE.**</u> Comenius proposed a *modern theory of discipline* in which the burden rests with the teacher to provide the interest and atmosphere in which the child will wish to learn. The child must understand the reason for rules. When all this fails, punishment must not be associated with schoolwork.

JOHN LOCKE

INTRODUCTION. John Locke was one of the most influential thinkers in history. *His political theory influenced the American and French Constitutions.* His views on education have contributed to the thoughts of every subsequent theorizer in the field.

LIFE OF LOCKE. Here follows a brief summary of the life of John Locke:

1. <u>**EARLY YOUTH.**</u> John Locke was *born near Bristol, England, in 1632.* His father was a successful *lawyer* and a man of comfortable means. Locke received a rudimentary education under the tutelage of his father, prior to entering the *Westminster School.* He studied the classics in preparation for Oxford. In *1652* he won a scholarship to *Christ College at Oxford.* During his time at Oxford, Locke was impressed by the thinking of *Rene Descartes.* This led him to an interest in science and medicine.

2. <u>**TEACHER, PHYSICIAN AND POLITICAL ADVISOR.**</u> Locke received a fellowship at Oxford in 1659. He taught both Greek and rhetoric. In 1666 he *decided to devote his life to medicine.* In treating the first Earl of Shaftesbury, Lord Ashley, he won his trust and admiration. Locke remained physician, tutor and political advisor to the Shaftesbury family until the Earl's death in 1683. However, Locke did not receive his degree in medicine from Oxford until 1674, because he refused for many years to acquiesce to the antiquated curriculum requirements of the university.

3. <u>**EXILE.**</u> Locke remained a Puritan his entire life. He supported the efforts of the Earl of Shaftesbury to prevent the Catholic Stuart, James II, from coming to the English Throne in succession to his brother, Charles II. This campaign failed. After James acceded to the throne, *Shaftesbury was arrested and tried for treason in 1681.* Although Shaftesbury was acquitted, both he and Locke went *into exile in Holland.* Shaftesbury died in that same year there. Locke went into hiding after James II demanded his extradition to stand trial for treason. Locke managed to live these years upon the *small monthly income* he received from his father's estate. When *William and Mary of Orange* captured the throne in 1688, Locke was free to return to England.

4. <u>**PHILOSOPHER.**</u> During his exile, Locke had been busy writing and studying philosophy. Shortly after his return to England in *1689* he published his first *Letter Con-*

cerning Toleration. The new regime offered Locke many lucrative posts, which he refused because of his poor health. He accepted the position of Commissioner of Appeals. *In 1690* he published his most famous work, *An Essay Concerning Human Understanding.* The same year witnessed the appearance of *Two Treatises on Government* and the second of four *Letters Concerning Toleration.* These works contributed to the great fame of John Locke during his own lifetime as the greatest English philosopher.

5. **EDUCATIONAL THEORY AND LAST YEARS.** In 1693, at the age of sixty-one, Locke published the series of letters which he had written to his friend, Edward Clarke, advising Clarke on the proper education of his son. These were called *"Some Thoughts Concerning Education."* Locke retired at the age of sixty-eight to the estate of his friends, Lord and Lady Masham. He died on October 28, 1704, famous throughout Europe. His thoughts were to inflame the philosophers of the Enlightenment and lead directly to the establishment of the democratic republic.

IMPORTANT PHILOSOPHICAL CONTRIBUTIONS. Among the many profound contributions made by John Locke, the following are important for educational theory:

1. **THE ACT OF KNOWING.** The mind at birth possesses no innate ideas. The mind of man is a *"tabula rasa" or blank slate* at birth, upon which is impressed many sense impressions. All knowledge proceeds through *sense experience.* As the mind stores up a variety of sense impressions, associations occur which provide new knowledge. *The mind* is consequently *passive. The senses provide the mind with the materials* which represent reality. These materials are not identical with the extramental object. *The material is the idea within the mind* which represents the object outside the mind being received by the senses. *By combining, comparing and analyzing* these materials or ideas arising through sensations, we derive thoughts. *Knowledge* is not sense perception but *intellectual perception.*

2. **RELIGIOUS TOLERATION.** Locke argued in his Letters Concerning Toleration that *no one religion* is capable of demonstrating its *exclusive claim* to be the one and true religion. It is wrong therefore to impose any one religion upon the *free consciences* of people. People ought to live in *complete tolerance* of one another's faiths.

3. **POLITICAL DEMOCRACY.** Governments were organized for the protection of all the citizens. Society was formed by the unanimous agreement of its members to live in one community for purposes of protection. The following represents some of *Locke's important political views:*

   a. <u>Government by the People.</u> The form a government takes derives from the consent of the majority of the citizens. Since all governments are created by the people, the *ultimate authority resides with the people* and not with the created government.

   b. <u>Protection.</u> Governments exist for the protection of the natural rights of every citizen. These are the rights of life, liberty and property. When any government attempts to remove these rights, this government becomes an unjust aggressor. No citizen ever gives up his natural rights. Therefore *the people have the right to resist* when a government abuses the powers entrusted to it. The act of resistance is not rebellion but self-defense.

EDUCATIONAL IMPLICATIONS OF LOCKE'S PHILOSOPHY. The following are some of the central points in Locke's educational theory:

1. **PURPOSE OF EDUCATION.** The purpose of education is to produce *an individual with a sound mind in a sound body*, so as to better serve his country.
2. **DIFFERENT CURRICULUM.** Locke thought that the content of education ought to depend upon *one's station in life. The common man* only required *moral, social and vocational knowledge.* He could do quite well with the Bible and a highly developed vocational skill that would serve to support him in life and offer social service to others. However, *the education of gentlemen* ought to be of the *very highest quality.* The gentleman must serve his country in a position of leadership.
3. **THE EDUCATION OF THE GENTLEMAN.** Locke believed that the gentleman must have a thorough knowledge of his own language. The schools of the Puritans in England broke with tradition completely. They sought *to educate one for the society in which he would live.* The schools were called, therefore, *schools of social realism.* Locke, in keeping *with Milton* and other Puritans, held that the *content* of the curriculum must serve some *practical end.* He recommended the introduction of *contemporary foreign languages, history, geography, economics, math and science.* Locke proposed the following for the education of the gentleman:

   a. **Moral Training.** All Christians must learn to live virtuously.
   b. **Good Breeding.** The gentleman must develop the *poise, control and outward behavior* of excellent manners. Education must aim, therefore, at developing correct social skills.
   c. **Wisdom.** The gentleman ought to *be able to apply intellectual and moral knowledge* in governing his practical affairs.
   d. **Useful Knowledge.** The gentleman must receive education which will lead to a successful life in the practical affairs of the society, as well as that which leads to the satisfaction derived from scholarship and good books.

11 | EDUCATION DURING THE ROMANTIC AGE

INTRODUCTION. In the late eighteenth and in the early nineteenth centuries, an educational movement which could be termed naturalistic, formed *the basis of modern educational theory and practice*. It served as the rationale for American social thought, in its emphasis upon *individuality and freedom*.

PHILOSOPHIC THEORY. The following principles reflect the major philosophical position of *Romanticism and Naturalism* during this period:

1. **EMOTION.** This philosophy stressed the role of feeling in the act of knowledge. Reason is inadequate because of its artificiality. Man must *experience fully the depth of emotion* to understand nature.
2. **NATURE.** The individual must become intensely interested in nature. He should intuit and feel the natural phenomena about him. *All things are good in a state of nature*. Nature is the highest value.
3. **NATURAL GOODNESS OF MAN.** The *formal restraints of society* may corrupt man. The closer man is to a state of nature, the more he becomes sincere, free and good. His imagination, emotion and passion is free to express itself in all its individuality.

JEAN JACQUES ROUSSEAU

THE LIFE OF ROUSSEAU. Jean Jacques Rousseau's life and work are described here in six parts:

1. **EARLY YOUTH.** Rousseau was born in Geneva, Switzerland on June 28, 1712. His family were pious Calvinists, refugees from France. A few days after his birth, *his mother died*. His father was a poor watchmaker and dancing-master. When Rousseau was ten, his father lost a legal battle with a rival. Sentenced to prison, *his father fled Geneva* leaving Jean Jacques to be raised by his wife's sister. Rousseau *left school at the age of twelve*. He was apprenticed to different trades with no success. Finally, *in 1728, he ran away* from Geneva.
2. **YEARS OF TRAVEL.** Shortly after leaving Geneva, Rousseau represented himself as a potential convert to a Catholic priest. After becoming a *Catholic convert*, he left Turin richer by twenty francs. He took service as a footman to a noblewoman, *Madame de Vercelli*. He revealed in his Confessions that he accused falsely a servant girl of giving him a stolen ribbon in order to escape punishment for stealing the ribbon. *Madame de Warens*, a wealthy widow, took him into her household. He lived with her as her kept lover for over nine years. She provided the means for him to receive a rudimentary classical education and a knowledge of music. In 1738 he left upon a journey to Montpellier to improve his health. He took a Madame de Larnage along with him. Upon his return to the country house of Madame de Warens outside of Chambery, he discovered that a man named Vintzenried had replaced him in the role of "amant en titre."

3. **LITERARY YEARS.** After an abortive attempt at teaching (a profession he thoroughly disliked), failure to obtain recognition for his system of musical notation and unsatisfactory service as secretary to the French Ambassador in Venice, *he returned to Paris in 1745.* He took *Therese le Vasseur,* a servant in his hotel, as his mistress. She is described as ugly, ignorant and illiterate. Yet they had *five children,* each of which was carried by Rousseau *to the Foundling Hospital* to be raised as orphans. *In 1749* Rousseau won the literary prize offered by the *Academy of Dijon* for an *essay* entitled, *"Discours sur les arts et sciences."* This essay won him great literary fame. Upon a visit to Geneva in 1754, Rousseau rejoined the Protestant Church and regained his citizenship rights.

4. **MAJOR WRITINGS.** In 1756 Rousseau moved into a cottage near Montmorency (famous as the "Hermitage"), established for him by Madame d'Epinay. In *1761* his novel *"La Nouvelle Heloise,"* which celebrated his love for Madame d'Houdetot, was published. He quarreled with Madame d'Epinay, with Diderot and the philosophy circle, and finally with Voltaire. Although in years to come he had many patrons, he fought with each one of them. In 1762 the political work *"The Social Contract"* and the novel *"Emile"* were published.

5. **EXILE.** The Social Contract, which favored the democratic city-state, and Emile, which recommended a natural religion, rejecting revelation and dogma, brought upon Rousseau the condemnation of the French Monarchy and the admiration of literary and philosophical circles in Europe. Forced to leave France, Rousseau was *befriended by Hume* in England. However, the growing mental illness of Rousseau reasserted itself and, thinking himself persecuted, he returned to France.

6. **LAST YEARS.** Rousseau returned to Paris in 1770. The next eight years were relatively peaceful. He wrote the *"Confessions," "Dialogues"* and *"Reveries du promeneur Solitaire."* An opera which he wrote, "Les Muses galantes," had been performed at the Paris Opera years earlier in 1747. In the closing years of his life, he wrote the fragments of another opera, *"Daphnis et Chloe."* This opera was published in 1780, following his death. A wealthy financier offered Rousseau the use of his cottage at Ermenonville in 1778. Suffering from his ┐psychological feelings of persecution, Rousseau accepted. The alcoholism and inclination for stable-boys of his mistress, Therese, heightened his problems. Rousseau had a stroke and *died on July 2, 1778.*

EDUCATIONAL CONTRIBUTIONS

EMILE. The greatest work produced by Rousseau is Emile. This work is more a tract upon education under the guise of a story than it is a novel in the true sense of the word novel. The book describes *the ideal education* which prepares Emile and Sophie for their eventual marriage. The following represents an *outline of the vital educational principles* found in Emile:

1. **BOOK ONE.** This book deals with *the infancy of the child.* The underlying thesis of all Rousseau's writings stresses *the natural goodness of man.* It is *society that corrupts* and makes a man evil. Rousseau states that the tutor can only stand by at this period of the child's development, ensuring that the child does not acquire any bad habits. Rousseau condemned the practice of some mothers who sent their infants to a wet nurse. He believed it was essential for *mothers to nurse their own children.* This practice is consistent with natural law.

2. **BOOK TWO.** Rousseau describes the education of the child when the tutor has full responsibility. Some of the major points of this section of the book are:

a. <u>Purpose of Education.</u> The tutor prepares the child for no particular social institution. Rather it is necessary *to preserve* the child *from* the baleful influence of *society. Education must be child-centered.* The tutor permits the child to develop his natural capacities. The aim of education is *never social.* It is always *individualistic.*

b. <u>The School.</u> Emile is educated away from city or town. Living in the country close to nature he should develop into the benevolent, good adult intended by nature. This school does not confine the youth to a classroom. No textbooks are utilized. The child learns by using his *senses in direct experience.*

c. <u>Problem Centered.</u> The tutor could employ *no force* in his teaching. When the child *felt the need* to know something, he would be moved to learn. Thus, Emile desired to know reading and writing in order to communicate with Sophie.

d. <u>Character Education.</u> The child learns morality by *experiencing the consequences* of his actions. Children are morally bad only after learning reprehensible behavior from adults. *Punishment is never resorted to* by the tutor.

e. <u>Physical Education.</u> Rousseau stresses the importance of physical activities in order to build a strong body. Emile is given opportunity to engage in swimming, running and athletic sports. *His diet and living conditions are rigidly controlled.* He lives in Spartan simplicity. (Rousseau was impressed and influenced by reading Plutarch's description of the life of the Spartan king, Lycurgus).

3. <u>BOOK THREE.</u> This section describes the intellectual education of Emile. Again, this education is based upon *Emile's own nature.* When he *is ready* to learn and *is interested* in language, geography, history and science, he will *possess the inner direction* necessary to learn. This learning would *grow out of the child's activities.* He will learn languages naturally through the normal conversational activity. Geography begins with the immediate surroundings of the youth and extends to the world through Emile's increased interest. The sense experience by which he observes the motion of the sun leads him to knowledge of astronomy. A knowledge of natural science is achieved through his interest in his own garden. *Rousseau* assumes that *Emile's motivation leads to the purposive self-discipline necessary to acquire knowledge.* Finally Emile is taught the *trade of carpentry* in order to prepare him for an occupation in life.

4. <u>BOOK FOUR.</u> This section describes *the social education and the religious education of Emile.* The education of Sophie is considered and the book concludes with the marriage of Emile and Sophie. The following represents some of the major points:

a. <u>Social Attitudes.</u> Emile is permitted to *mingle with people in society at the age of sixteen.* He is guided toward the desireable attitudes that lead to self-respect. Emile's earlier education protects him from the corrupting influence of society.

b. <u>Natural Religion.</u> The revelation and dogma of organized religion are unnecessary for man. The fundamental tenets of any religion affirm the existence of God and the immortality of the soul. These are *known through the heart* only. It is not only unnecessary, but impossible to reason to these truths. The Savoyard Vicar explains this natural religion, as Emile experiences the sensitive emotion derived from his view of the valley of the Po. Religion, therefore, is *a matter of personal feeling and emotion.*

c. <u>Education of Women.</u> Having completed the explanation of Emile's ideal education, Rousseau turns his attention to the education of Sophie. Women are not educated as are men. *The natural purpose of a woman is to please a man.*

She is expected to have and care for children, and to please, advise and console her husband whenever necessary. Her education does not extend beyond this purpose.

JOHANN BERNARD BASEDOW

INTRODUCTION. The educational theories of Basedow were *similar to those of Rousseau.* Beyond a doubt the reading of Emile influenced Basedow in the application of naturalism to education. However, Basedow had expressed many similar ideas prior to the publication of Emile. The points upon which Basedow and Rousseau differ are important. Basedow believed in *schools reformed with his new methods.* The *socialization processes of education* are important in the school of Basedow in contrast to the individualized tutorial education of Emile. Basedow is an original educator in his own right. He is the major *reformer of the school system of Germany.*

LIFE OF BASEDOW. The major events in the life of Basedow may be summarized thus:

1. <u>EARLY YOUTH.</u> Basedow was *born in 1723 in Hamburg,* Germany. His mother was insane. His father worked as a wigmaker. Basedow *revolted against the learning by rote and cruel discipline* of the grammar school. Leaving school, he idled away his time among the ruffians of the town. When he was an adolescent he ran away from home and worked as a servant in the home of a physician.

2. <u>EDUCATION.</u> Recognizing the brilliant mind of the youth, *the doctor persuaded Basedow to return to school.* Basedow returned to grammar school. The teachers in the upper grades recommended him for the University, overlooking his unruly and undisciplined behavior in favor of his keen intelligence. In 1744 Basedow entered the *University of Leipzig* to study for the ministry.

3. <u>YOUNG ADULT YEARS.</u> During the two years that Basedow spent in the University, he *rarely attended any lectures* or pursued the study of philosophy and religion in an organized fashion. He *wrote term papers for money* for students who lacked ability. Basedow acquired additional funds by tutoring wealthy students. Then he spent his money in riotous living in the city.

4. <u>TEACHER.</u> Basedow accepted a position as tutor to an aristocratic child in 1749. Concentrating on *the child's interest in play,* Basedow developed many ingenious games by which he taught his charge. Language was taught through conversation rather than the common learning by rote approach. When the young aristocrat was ten years old, he was able to read and write German and Latin. He had an adult grasp upon arithmetic, geography, history and science. Much of this was attributed to *Basedow's creative teaching methods.*

5. <u>UNIVERSITY OF SURO.</u> As a result of Basedow's success in teaching, he was given an appointment in philosophy at the Danish University of Suro. As a professor, Basedow was immensely successful in teaching and unsuccessful to the same degree in faculty relations. His brilliant and interesting lectures won him great *popularity among the students.* His immoderate life in the town, tendency to brag and attacks upon organized religion won him *enemies among the faculty.* After eight years Basedow was *expelled by governmental order.*

6. <u>GYMNASIUM AT ALTONA.</u> Basedow was appointed as Gymnasium teacher in Altona. Here Basedow *failed to win any success.* The aristocratic students disliked him. The administration reduced his teaching hours and the point was reached where he was assigned no class whatever. Basedow took this opportunity to write. *His treatises attacked the established religions* and won him many new enemies.

7. <u>EDUCATIONAL MONOGRAPH.</u> In 1768 Basedow published a monograph on education setting forth his plans for the improvement of education. This won him great fame at the time. Basedow suggested in this work that *a laboratory school be established to implement new methods* and provide a training ground for pre-service teachers. Basedow felt the *need for an encyclopedia in education* which would guide every teacher in the use of proper methods and curricula.

8. <u>"ELEMENTARY BOOK."</u> Basedow raised enough money through public subscription to begin the "Elementary Book." In 1770 he published the first part of this work. *Part I* dealt with *teaching methods*. Toward the end of his labors in Part II, Basedow accepted the help of another educator named *Wolke*. *Part II*, which presented a complete *curriculum* for the schools, was published in 1772.

9. <u>THE SCHOOL IN DESSAU.</u> In 1771 the Prince of Anhalt offered to support a school in Dessau if Basedow would organize and administer the school. This school, called the "Philanthropinum," began in 1774 with fifteen pupils. A *public examination* of these young scholars, held in 1776, impressed learned observers who arrived for the event from all over Europe. *Basedow failed as an administrator* as the years passed. His excessive drinking and violent outbursts of emotion drove away the better teachers (including his friend Wolke), and brought on a negligent teaching atmosphere. Although *Basedow had left the school by 1785*, the administrative damage led to the termination of Dessau as a school in 1793.

10. <u>LAST YEARS.</u> Basedow became enthusiastic about introducing *a new method of reading.* In 1785 he became a volunteer teacher at Magdeburg in order to try out his system of teaching reading. *Basedow died in 1790* of a cerebral hemorrhage.

EDUCATIONAL CONTRIBUTION OF BASEDOW. The work of Basedow brought educational reforms to the schools of Germany. His curriculum stressed *the importance of the vernacular in education* and led to the elimination of the former Latin grammar schools. His recommendations increased the study of science in the schools. The methodology which he advocated demanded that teachers *stimulate and interest the pupils*. Games were introduced to encourage the learning of pupils by playing upon their interests. He *removed all memorization by rote* from the teaching of languages and replaced it with a natural conversational method. Cruel physical punishment disappeared as a result of his writings, and teaching became a profession of trained professionals. The sense realism in Basedow's method anticipates the modern method of teaching.

SCHOOLS DURING THE SEVENTEENTH AND EIGHTEENTH CENTURIES. The types of schools that dominated the educational scene during the seventeenth and eighteenth centuries were:

1. <u>PARISH SCHOOLS.</u> In Catholic nations there existed a very large number of schools attached to parish churches in villages or to individual parishes within the cities. These schools were taught by religious orders of men and women, who devoted their lives to God through teaching. The *Jesuit schools were outlawed in England and France.* This led to:

   a. <u>The Hedge School.</u> In England and Ireland mainly, priests hiding from the law taught small groups outside of school buildings.

   b. <u>Christian Brothers.</u> There was an increase in the number of schools run by Christian Brothers. Jean Baptiste de la Salle (1661-1719) had established the *Society of the Brothers of the Christian Schools*. This was a *community of lay teachers* who lived the religious life of teaching Brothers. Their schools spread throughout Europe and have continued through the years until the present day.

2. **VILLAGE SCHOOLS.** Many villages throughout Europe provided for a primary elementary school where Church schools did not exist. These schools stressed *the basics of reading, writing and arithmetic*. The girls were taught some domestic skills. In Germany the elementary education *eliminated Latin* entirely from the curriculum. These elementary schools are referred to as *Vernacular Schools*.
3. **WORKHOUSE SCHOOLS.** The English Parliament passed a *"Poor Law" in 1601* to help eliminate poverty and idleness. This law placed a tax upon the people in order to provide work for the poor and to found *vocational schools* in which the children of the poor would learn a skill for future employment. These schools usually taught some rudimentary reading, writing and arithmetic.
4. **THE DAME SCHOOL.** This type of school was unique to England. Each was a private school, *held in the home of a woman*, in which a small number of young children were taught *reading and etiquette*.

PESTALOZZI

INTRODUCTION. The influence of Pestalozzi was enormous *throughout Western civilization*. His methods were adopted in Prussia, making their school system one of the best in the world during the nineteenth century. American educators studied these schools in order to evoke educational reform at home. Teacher training was improved in France. *Only in England was his influence lost*. Except for the aristocracy, English education lagged behind the rest of Europe.

LIFE. The following facts represent the major events in the life of Pestalozzi:

1. **EARLY YOUTH.** Pestalozzi was *born in Zurich, Switzerland on January 12, 1746*. His father died when he was five, and he was raised in a loving home consisting of his mother, older sister and woman servant. He did not enter school until he was nine. His *elementary school record was not impressive* because of his tendency to daydream. However, he did enter and complete his studies at the *University of Zurich*. He began as a student for the ministry, but his shyness led him away from theology and into law.
2. **FARM AT NEUHOF.** Desirous of alleviating the hardship of *poverty among the masses*, Pestalozzi began a social experiment in which he hoped to make his newly purchased farm a *center of humanistic activity*. He married his childhood friend. She helped him to temper many of his more impractical ideas. Pestalozzi learned his teaching methods from his experiences in teaching his son, Jacobi. *These methods were inspired by reading Emile*. Later they were changed with additional experience. Pestalozzi took in a group of orphans and vagrant or abandoned children. The instruction he gave those children was very successful. He went bankrupt in 1780 after five years of this social experiment. His small family was saved from starvation by the services of a kindly servant neighbor, *Elizabeth Naef*. Elizabeth managed the farm with such success that the Pestalozzis were never again in want.
3. **WRITER AND TEACHER.** Pestalozzi wrote the novel *Leonard and Gertrude* in 1781. This book, incorporating many of Pestalozzi's ideas about educational and social reform, became an educational classic. Its publication brought Pestalozzi fame but no alleviation from hard work and near poverty on the farm. He published the book *"Fables"* in 1791, which was a collection of animal stories with simple

morals. The same year witnessed the writing of his *"Inquiry."* This philosophical work was a failure.

4. <u>**ORPHANAGE AT STANZ.**</u> His offer to assist the orphaned children of Stanz, following the widespread destruction caused by the Swiss revolution, was accepted. For five months he labored continually and successfully in spite of religious and educational criticism. *The orphanage was closed after another war.*

5. <u>**SCHOOL AT BURGDORF.**</u> Pestalozzi volunteered his services without pay to the village of Burgdorf. The villagers were suspicious of his methods, and it became evident that it would be *necessary for him to establish his own private school.* He was assisted in this by another schoolmaster, named *Krusi.* With two additional teachers, they began together *the school which attracted international attention and fame.* Pestalozzi won government support as his fame increased. He published in 1801 a systematic treatise on education, *"How Gertrude Teaches Her Children."* He moved his school to a castle at Yverdon in 1805.

6. <u>**LAST YEARS.**</u> The school at Yverdon lasted for twenty years. It attracted students and teachers from many nations in its early days. Representatives from Prussia returned home to change and improve their educational system. As the institution grew in size, *some of the teachers changed the methods of Pestalozzi and quarrels resulted,* creating dissension and wholesale resignations. Pestalozzi remained with the school until the very end. When the school closed in 1826, *Pestalozzi, then a man of eighty, retired to his farm.* His remaining time involved him in invective disputes with some of his former teachers. *He died February 17, 1827.*

PESTALOZZIAN PRINCIPLES OF EDUCATION. Some of the very many principles of Pestalozzi's education can be summed up as follows:

1. <u>**EDUCATION.**</u> Education is the *unfolding of the natural powers and faculties latent in every human being.*

2. <u>**PURPOSE OF EDUCATION.**</u> The purpose of education is *both social and individual.* Education provides the means for the social regeneration of humanity. As the moral, social, emotional and intellectual development of each individual unfolds through education, society is also improved by these individuals who achieve their full potential.

3. <u>**THE CURRICULUM.**</u> The curriculum of the elementary school was enlarged to include *geography, science (through the study of nature), drawing and music.*

4. <u>**METHODOLOGY.**</u> The following are the chief points of Pestalozzi's method:

    a. <u>**Child Centered.**</u>

    b. <u>**Direct Experience.**</u> The teacher must never teach by words when a child can see, hear or touch an object for himself. *Nature can teach the child better than man can.*

    c. <u>**Activity.**</u> The child is expected to be *continually active* in seeing for himself, making and correcting mistakes, describing his observations, analyzing objects and satisfying his natural curiosity.

    d. <u>**Induction.**</u> The child must observe, learn to express his impressions of concrete objects perceived by the senses and must learn to formulate new generalizations for himself.

    e. <u>**No Books.**</u> Early elementary education needs *direct and concrete experience* rather than books. In this way the child proceeds from the concrete to the abstract.

    f. <u>**Simplify All Subjects.**</u> All subjects are reduced to their simple *elements.* The child proceeds, through experiencing the simple parts, to formulate more abstract generalizations.

5. DISCIPLINE. Pestalozzi asserted that *the teacher must earn the trust of the children*. He advocated a policy of "thinking love" in handling children. The schoolroom must possess the atmosphere of a loving Christian family. The members of this family are *cooperative, loving and kind* to one another. Pestalozzi deplored the harsh treatment of children which was widespread during this period of history. He felt that restrictive measures limit the teacher-pupil relationship and prevent the natural development of children and that this is especially true in moral matters.

INFLUENCE OF PESTALOZZI. In addition to being a great influence upon the elementary school system of Prussia, he influenced American education. The superintendent of schools in Oswego, New York, *Dr. Edward A. Sheldon,* imported the materials developed in England and Canada from Pestalozzi. This led to the establishment of a *teacher normal school* to prepare teachers in the application of Pestalozzi's method. The Normal School *at Oswego* (established in 1861), became the center of Pestalozzi education in the United States. An investigation of this school by the N.E.A. in 1865 resulted in a favorable report. This led to changes elsewhere in the country. The future normal schools that developed throughout the West adopted the Oswego plan. As new teachers rose to administrative positions in the United States, the teachings of Pestalozzi became active in countless school systems.

12 | EUROPEAN EDUCATION IN THE NINETEENTH CENTURY

JOHANN FRIEDRICH HERBART

INTRODUCTION. The ideas of Herbart had a *significant impact upon American education* during the late nineteenth and early twentieth centuries. His views stimulated the application of psychology to pedagogy and the systematic preparation of teachers. It placed history and literature in the curriculum of elementary American education.

LIFE. The following are the chief events in the life of Johann Friedrich Herbart:

1. **EARLY YOUTH.** Herbart was *born May 4, 1776, in Oldenburg, Germany*. His family were prominent people in Oldenburg. Herbart received his early tutoring from his mother. He did not enter the Gymnasium until he was twelve years of age. He was an exceptionally bright student who graduated with honors in 1794. The same year he graduated found him entering the *University of Jena* as a law student. Finding law not to his taste, Herbart left the University and accepted a *position as tutor* to the three sons of the Governor of *Interlaken, Switzerland*, in 1797. During the three years he served as tutor, Herbart *visited Pestalozzi* at Burgdorf.
2. **COLLEGE TEACHER.** Herbart became a lecturer on education and philosophy at the *University of Gottingen in 1802*. His great educational treatise, *"The Science of Education,"* was published in 1806. In 1808 he became a *professor of Philosophy* at the *University of Konigsberg*, occupying the Chair of Philosophy formerly held by Immanuel Kant. Herbart established teacher training and teaching seminars at Konigsberg. His purpose was to make *education a science based upon psychology*. His meeting with Pestalozzi was significant in his life. Herbart formulated a philosophical and psychological synthesis for Pestalozzi's method. He returned to the University of Gottingen in 1833 as a philosophy professor. He published *The Outlines of Educational Doctrine*. On *August 14, 1841, he died* of a stroke, shortly after delivering a lecture.

INFLUENCE OF HERBART. Herbartian ideas had much influence upon education:

1. **SPREAD OF HIS IDEAS.** In 1865 *Professor Tuiskon Ziller* of the University of Leipzig popularized the educational ideas of Herbart. A student of Ziller's, *Professor William Rein*, established *a center* for study of Herbartian ideas at the *University of Jena*. This center influenced education throughout Germany.
2. **AMERICAN EDUCATORS.** Some American educators from the Illinois State Normal School at Bloomington, Illinois, studied education at Jena. Of these educators, Charles De Garmo published *The Essentials of Method* in 1889, Charles McMurry published the *General Method* in 1892, and Charles and Frank McMurry published *The Method of the Recitation* in 1897. These method books, along with the writings of the Herbartian Society, influenced American education.

3. **THE HERBARTIAN SOCIETIES.** The first Herbartian Society was organized in Germany in 1868 for the study and improvement of the science of education. The National Herbartian Society was organized in America in 1892. This society evolved into the *National Society for the Study of Education or the N.S.S.E.*, with two publications a year published by the University of Chicago Press.

EDUCATIONAL CONTRIBUTIONS OF HERBART. These are some of the important theories in education found in the works of Herbart:

1. **PURPOSE OF EDUCATION.** Influenced by Immanuel Kant, Herbart believed that moral imperatives required all human beings to obey their consciences and to do their moral duty. The *highest aim* of education, therefore, is the *development of a sound character* in every child, with which he will possess the *strength of will to do what is right.*

2. **ASSOCIATIONISTIC PSYCHOLOGY.** Herbart declared that each individual learned by building up many sense impressions of external objects. When these simple impressions become associated with other perceptions, the mind or consciousness is formed. These perceptions become associated in complex combinations. The combinations are termed an *apperceptive mass* of experience. The structure of the human mind is made up of these apperceptive masses. When a new experience is assimilated by the mind, it is transformed by the apperceptive mass of past experience into a new apperception. Not all perceptions remain in the consciousness. *Some perceptions are stored in the unconscious* and recalled with the occurrence of a new associated experience. *Learning requires:*

   a. **Sense Experience**
   b. **Progress from the Known to The Unknown**
   c. **Experiential Readiness**
   d. **Interest Based on Prior Experience.**

3. **THE TEACHING PROCESS.** It is necessary for the teacher to keep in mind the *five formal steps* in the learning process. These steps are:

   a. **Preparation.** The learner must be *interested and attentive* in the lesson. The teacher must begin by achieving this through clarifying the objectives of the lesson, building the lesson from the learner's past experience and relating the lesson to prior experiences.
   b. **Presentation.** All new materials must be *based upon what the learner already knows.* The new experiences must then be arranged from the concrete and simple to the abstract and complex.
   c. **Association.** In this step, the learner is provided with the opportunity of *perceiving the relationships* that exist between the new material and prior learnings. The teacher must analyze the content and describe the relationships in order to create an intellectual climate in which the new material will fit in with prior perceptive masses.
   d. **Generalization.** The learner must *seek new meanings or principles* based upon prior relations or associations in the material to be learned.
   e. **Application.** In this step, the learner enriches his knowledge of new principles *by testing them and applying them* to new situations.

4. **THE CURRICULUM.** Herbart stressed the importance of literature and history in the curriculum because his ultimate purpose in education *was the development*

of a sound moral character. The contact man has with his fellow men in social intercourse provides the core of studies by which the learner is afforded opportunity in developing a sound moral character. *A person is naturally interested in people.* This aspect of the curriculum, therefore, is based upon the natural interest of man. Man is also interested in his environment. So the curriculum must include, though they are less important, the *study of concepts* found in science, mathematics and the arts.

INTRODUCTION. The man who founded the kindergarten movement, with its emphasis upon individual liberty and worth, self-discovery through self-activity, and group activity as a means of desirable social development, influenced elementary education everywhere. This man was Friedrich Froebel.

FRIEDRICH WILHELM AUGUST FROEBEL

LIFE OF FROEBEL. His life and significant events in it are summarized below:

1. **EARLY YOUTH.** Friedrich Froebel was born in *Oberwiessbach, Germany, April 21, 1782.* His father was a Lutheran minister. His mother died when he was in his infancy. After his father remarried, *life became harsh* for young Friedrich. His stepmother, interested in her own child, thought unkindly of Friedrich. With all his older brothers away at school, life was lonely for him until he was sent to live with a kind uncle. He attended school during this time.
2. **UNIVERSITY OF JENA.** After a visit to his older brother, a medical student at Jena, Froebel determined to study at this university. His family thought him incapable of any intellectual achievements. So Froebel continued in the practical studies designed to equip him as a *forester.* At Jena, Froebel came under the influence of *the philosophies of Fichte and Schelling.* These pantheistic philosophers were the forerunners of a romanticism which stressed the search for one's inner unity in order to interpret all of reality. Unfortunately for Froebel, *he fell into debt* after lending an older brother money which was not repaid. His father paid the debts and liberated Froebel from prison only after his son agreed to sign away all rights to his father's inheritance.
3. **TEACHER.** Froebel failed at a number of inconsequential jobs. At one time he wished to become an architect but lacked the funds necessary to continue his studies. He received an offer to teach drawing at Frankfurt. With no prior training in education, Froebel became *an immediate success as a teacher.* After two years he accepted a position as tutor to three boys. Influenced by Rousseau, he began the tutorial work in the country. Subsequently, he enrolled with his three charges at *the school of Pestalozzi* in Yverdon, Switzerland. He soon became an enthusiastic supporter of Pestalozzi. When the three boys were ready for university, Froebel enrolled at the *University of Gottingen.* He enlisted in the German army in 1813 and fought in the German war for independence against Napoleon. While in the army he made a life-long friendship with *Heinrich Langethal and Wilhelm Middendorff.*
4. **THE UNIVERSAL GERMAN INSTITUTE.** Froebel determined to become an educator in 1816. He walked from Berlin to Keilhau to see the widow of his brother. She agreed to finance a school for him with the tacit understanding of future marriage. Together with Middendorff and Langethal, he began the school with five pupils (three of whom were his nephews, sons of the widow). When the school had prospered, Froebel married a wealthy Berliner. This caused him embarrassment later on in Switzerland when his nephews attacked him in print.

5. **THE KINDERGARTEN.** Froebel published *"The Education of Man"* in 1826. During an interlude of teaching in Switzerland, he came into contact with orphans in Burgdorf. This developed his idea of a *need for pre-school experiences* for the very young. After a study of nursery schools in Berlin, he opened his *"Kindergarten" in Blankenburg.* Despite the loss of his wife, he continued for seven years to labor at this work.

6. **LAST YEARS.** When he was sixty-two years old, Froebel attempted to spread his idea of the kindergarten all over Germany. He began a training school for young women who wished to teach in the kindergarten. He married one of his early students, *Luise Levin*, thirty years his junior. Together they travelled through Germany *giving demonstrations* of the play and songs of the Kindergarten. He won the support of important aristocrats such as the Baroness von Marenholtz-Bulow. Kindergartens and schools for kindergarten teachers were established in many places. In the year of his death, 1852, Froebel, then seventy years of age, attended the National Convention of German teachers, where his work was eulogized. *He died peacefully on June 21, 1852.*

7. **CONCLUSION.** The first English-speaking kindergarten in America was a private school opened by the sister-in-law of *Horace Mann*, Elizabeth Peabody, *in Boston in 1860.* Five years earlier a German-speaking kindergarten had been opened by a pupil of Froebel in Watertown, Wisconsin. *In 1873 the first Kindergarten attached to a public school system opened in St. Louis* through the efforts of Superintendent *William Torrey Harris.* Within seven years, four hundred public kindergartens were in full operation. At the turn of the century, 4,500 kindergartens existed. *Dewey adopted Froebel's principles* in his laboratory school in the University of Chicago. Francis W. Parker led the movement to implement the ideas and ideals of Froebel in American elementary education. Today elementary schools across America are less rigid, less harsh, more concerned with individual differences and socialization of the child because of Froebel.

FROEBEL'S PRINCIPLES OF EDUCATION. Some of the important ideas and ideals of Froebel in education were:

1. **THE PURPOSE OF EDUCATION.** The aim of education is to develop the inner capacities and abilities of each child so that all his potentialities will be realizable as an adult. *The whole child* must develop through *creative self-expression* in order that he may become a socially active adult in all the aspirations of humanity.

2. **PRINCIPLES OF METHODOLOGY.** The following represent some of Froebel's ideas which serve as a guide to methodology in teaching:

    a. the child learns by doing,
    b. the "inner unfolding" of the child occurs through self activity,
    c. child growth and development through spontaneous activities,
    d. the child learns social cooperation through the social environment of the classroom,
    e. freedom for the child permits the development of curiosity and the organization of his natural energies,
    f. all learning must be child centered,
    g. the child learns through play activities,
    h. the child must feel the need for an educational activity,
    i. the whole child must be afforded the opportunity to develop his intellectual, physical, emotional, social, and moral self.

3. <u>CURRICULUM.</u> Froebel recommended an *Activity Curriculum.* Play materials were provided and organized in a systematic manner to insure growth and progress. These materials he called *"gifts."* Games stressing both individual skill and co-operative activity should be available. Froebel advocated nature study when the child's interests led in this direction. Art materials of every type and musical instruments and books should be available to the child.

EDUCATIONAL DEVELOPMENTS AT THE CLOSE OF THE NINETEENTH CENTURY

INTRODUCTION. Social changes during the nineteenth century had enormous effects upon education throughout Western civilization. *Some of these major social changes were:*

1. <u>THE GROWTH OF DEMOCRACY</u>
2. <u>INDUSTRIAL REVOLUTION</u>
3. <u>GREAT SCIENTIFIC PROGRESS</u>
4. <u>STATE CONTROL OF PUBLIC EDUCATION</u>
5. <u>WORLDWIDE COMMERCE</u>
6. <u>CAPITALISTIC WEALTH</u>
7. <u>THE GROWTH OF HUGE CITIES</u>

HERBERT SPENCER

INTRODUCTION. The writings of Spencer had *tremendous influence in the United States.* The Spencerian emphasis upon practicality, science and educational preparation for comfortable living were influential in the adoption of science and elective courses in both colleges and secondary schools in the United States.

LIFE OF SPENCER. This is a summary of Spencer's life and work:

1. <u>EARLY YOUTH.</u> Herbert Spencer was *born April 27, 1820, in Derby, England.* He received no formal education until he was thirteen. At this time he was sent to study at Hinton, much against his will. He remained a student there until 1836. These *three years constitute the sum total of his formal education* because Spencer refused the offer of his uncle to support him through the University of Cambridge.
2. <u>ADULT.</u> Spencer worked on the railroads in Birmingham and Gloucester between 1837 and 1841. When he was twenty-one years old, he resigned his position as a railroad engineer in favor of journalism. In 1848 Spencer became a subeditor of the *Economist.* He resigned in 1853, when a legacy from his uncle provided him with some independence. *The theme of his writings was individualism.* His individuality and sense of freedom was so intense that *his economic and social theory of government* could be described as extremely *laissez-faire.*
3. <u>WRITER.</u> While Spencer was still editing on the Economist, he published the *Social Statics* in 1851. This was his first book. It contained many views which he elaborated upon in the years to come. When Spencer wrote this work he had read only one book on the subject. He published the first part of his *The Principles of Psychology* in 1857. In 1860 Spencer began the comprehensive *Synthetic Philosophy,* which was not completed until the publication of the third volume of *Principles of Sociology* in 1896. Spencer viewed philosophy as the effort to integrate or synthesize into a whole frame of reference all of the descriptions of the sciences. Spen-

cer was the first since Francis Bacon to attempt a complete synthesis of all of knowledge. Also in 1860 there appeared under the general title *"Education"* four monographs he had written on this subject. His *First Principles*, published in 1862, presented a philosophy of evolution. Spencer believed that an unknown and unknowable force exists in the universe. This accounts for the variety underlying all development. Although he subsequently accepted Darwin's idea of Natural Selection, he retained his belief in the inherited acquired characteristics as an explanation for evolution. His *Principles of Biology*, which appeared in 1864, advanced the concept of "survival of the fittest" in evolutionary theory. Spencer *died December 8, 1904, in Brighton, England*, recognized as one of the foremost thinkers of the nineteenth century.

EDUCATIONAL THEORY OF HERBERT SPENCER. His important ideas and purposes in education were:

1. **THE PURPOSE OF EDUCATION.** The aim of all education is to prepare the individual for *complete living in this life*. According to him, the functions of living are:

   a. **Self-preservation and Health**
   b. **Vocational Competency**
   c. **Parenthood**
   d. **Citizenship**
   e. **Use of Leisure Time.**

2. **METHODOLOGY.** Spencer agreed with many of the thinkers in education regarding teaching method:

   a. **Teaching.** Teaching involves a procedure of going from the known to the unknown.
   b. **Learning.** Learning takes place through individual interest.
   c. **Social Behavior.** Social behavior is learned by the individual through experiencing the consequences of his actions.

3. **CURRICULUM.** Spencer stressed *the study of science* in order to meet the needs of self preservation, vocational skill, parenthood, citizenship and leisure time. The *social sciences* are particularly relevant in parenthood, citizenship and leisure time. *Mathematics* has practical use in providing knowledge necessary for vocational competency. Spencer acknowledged the practical application the fine arts have in meeting the needs of every human being in utilizing his leisure time effectively. The sole criterion for an educational curriculum is, therefore, the usefulness the subjects have in the life of the student.

SEGUIN, BINET AND MONTESSORI

INTRODUCTION. The teaching of *handicapped children* received great impetus in Europe and then in America through the work of Edouard Seguin in motor activity, Alfred Binet in psychological testing, and Maria Montessori in teaching method.

EDUCATIONAL CONTRIBUTIONS OF EDOUARD SEGUIN (1812-1880). Under the influence of Saint Simon, who hoped for the social advancement of all, Seguin worked as a physician with extreme mental defectives. Seguin made the following contributions to education:

1. **TEACHING TECHNIQUE.** He developed a successful *technique for the education of idiots.* He demonstrated his ability to train idiots to take care of their bodily needs, speak understandably and use their senses.
2. **SENSORY DEFICIENCY.** Seguin based his method upon the assumption that the mind of an idiot is sound. However, the idiot's *sensory equipment is deficient* in some way. As a result of this, outside stimuli are not readily received by the brain. Futhermore, the sensory deficiency extends to the inability of the idiot to coordinate his muscular movements.
3. **PHYSICAL TRAINING.** He developed a *walking-machine* to train exceptional idiot children to acquire independent motion. The principle of this machine is used in the training of paraplegics today.
4. **MENTAL TRAINING.** Seguin trained the *faculty of imitation* in order to develop the simple potentialities of the child.

EDUCATIONAL CONTRIBUTIONS OF ALFRED BINET (1857-1911). Binet's greatest contribution to the world of education was in the field of *psychology.* The following are some of his important contributions:

1. **INTELLIGENCE QUOTIENT.** He developed a *scale for the measurement of intelligence.* I.Q. measurement began with Binet's work to assist a commission studying the education of mentally defective children in 1904.
2. **METHOD.** Education must be based upon *the experimental method* of science. Binet was *highly critical of method* books in education. Each child is an individual who must be observed, known and taught according to his abilities and aptitudes. Many books in educational methodology assume a common ideal method for the teaching of everyone. The Binet measurement of intelligence is always an *individual test* in which the tester wins the confidence and trust of the child before proceeding through a series of game-like activities to assess the place of the child upon the ladder of intelligence.
3. **MENTAL AGE.** Binet developed the *concept of mental age* as opposed to chronological age. This pointed to the *individual* differences existing between each child in a given classroom.
4. **LEVELS.** Binet also produced a *classification and description* for each level of intellectual development from the idiot through genius.

EDUCATIONAL CONTRIBUTIONS OF MARIA MONTESSORI (1870-1952). Montessori established a school that became the prototype of hundreds of similar schools throughout Europe and America. The following represent some of her important contributions:

1. **RETARDED CHILDREN.** Montessori established the *Orthophrenic School* for feeble-minded and defective children in 1898.
2. **NORMAL CHILDREN.** In 1917 Montessori established the *"Casa du Bambini"* in Rome. This school implemented her methods for the teaching of *normal children.*
3. **METHOD.** Montessori introduced a method which stressed the *individual freedom* of each child to function at his own level of development, utilizing *structured teaching materials and games.* These materials were designed to provide for the development of the child's senses. The educational work was both *manual and intellectual.*
4. **THEORY.** Montessori's educational theory assumes that the child must be provided with the maximum amount of *liberty.* The *teacher motivates and guides* the child in the *self-development* of social, emotional and intellectual tasks which are necessary for its self-realization.

5. <u>PRINCIPLES.</u> Some of the principles of Montessori education are:

a. The child learns with his senses as well as his intellect.

b. <u>Success.</u> Success in learning *rewards* the child and breeds confidence.

c. <u>Curriculum.</u> Educational activities should *never be forced. Each child selects whatever activity* appeals to him. He proceeds according to his interests and abilities.

d. <u>Motivation.</u> The child *learns for himself* whatever he needs for his own independence.

e. <u>Classes.</u> The school is *ungraded.*

f. <u>Block of time and team teaching are necessary.</u> The block of time permits the child to pursue his tasks without interruption.

g. <u>Responsibility and Communication.</u> The child *develops a sense of morality and social responsibility by himself at his own pace.* Adults never teach children responsibility by word. *Communication* between the adult and the child is *upon the unconscious feeling level.* The child senses what the adult is.

h. <u>Teaching.</u> Teaching must be always *child centered.* The activities follow from the nature of the child.

i. <u>Learning.</u> The child will learn when he is *ready* physically and experientially to learn.

j. <u>Development of Personality.</u> The structured *environment* of the child exists to *reveal the child* and never to shape or mold him.

EDUCATION IN THE UNITED STATES

COLONIAL BEGINNINGS. The major influences upon American education came from England. The school system of any society reflects the dominant forces in that society. *Colonial American society* was divided as follows:

1. <u>NEW ENGLAND.</u> The colonists of the Massachusetts Bay Colony were religious dissenters who had established *a theocratic society* along Calvinistic lines. Their religion demanded that they have the ability to read the Bible. This led to the *first state-controlled education* in the English-speaking world. Here is a description of their main institutes of education:

    a. <u>Harvard College.</u> It was founded in 1636. The first universities in the New World had been established a century earlier in Mexico City, and in Lima, Peru. *The first college in the English Colonies was established by public funds* in the Bay Colony. The Reverend John Harvard bequeathed his estate to this college which was being built in present-day Cambridge, Massachusetts. When the college was named, it was called Harvard after its benefactor. Its major function was the training of future clergymen. It adopted the curriculum of Cambridge University, England. Although the College *began as a public institution, it received a private charter* in 1650.

    b. <u>Boston Latin School.</u> *A Latin grammar school was established in Boston in 1636.* This school adopted the curriculum of the English schools. It trained boys between the ages of eight and fifteen for Harvard. This school became the *prototype* of similar schools which grew throughout New England. By the year 1700, there existed twenty-six such schools. These schools existed for boys only.

    c. <u>The Law of 1642.</u> The Colony passed a law in 1642 requiring *the selectmen of the various towns* to ensure that all children were educated sufficiently to read the principles of religion and the laws of the land.

    d. <u>The Old Deluder Satan Law of 1647.</u> This Law required every community having *at least fifty homes* to provide *primary elementary instruction* for every boy and girl. The purpose of the Law was to insure the fact that every citizen would be literate enough to read the Bible and thereby frustrate the wiles of Satan.

    e. <u>The New England Primer.</u> This basic textbook in reading *appeared in 1690.* It contained religious moral *truths for each letter of the alphabet.* The readings were entirely moralistic. This book was in use through the eighteenth century.

    f. <u>The Moving School.</u> As the Colony grew in size and the government became less fanatical, *roving schoolmasters* wandered through the various towns spending a few months in each town. This condition existed throughout the Thirteen Colonies. However, in New England the established schools still remained. *In 1701* a group of Conservative Congregational ministers *founded Yale* College to preserve the Faith.

2. **THE SOUTH.** The Colonists of the South were *loyal to the Church of England.* The educational policies followed those found in England. However, geographic and economic conditions made the parish school impossible in a region with a widely-scattered population living on plantations. *Education in the South was* characterized by the following types:

a. **Private Tutor.** The large majority of wealthy children were educated by private family tutors.

b. **Apprentice Schools.** The children of the poor, orphans and young mulattoes were provided with a certain amount of basic training in some of the Colonies. This began with the *Virginia Law of 1641 (similar to the English Poor Laws), to ensure some type of work skills for the poor.*

c. **Workhouse Schools.** The laws of 1668 and 1705 in Virginia were important in that workhouse schools were required to be built by public funds for the *training of children of the poor.* In 1705 the law demanded that these schools *include reading and writing* in their curricula.

d. **The College of William and Mary.** The cornerstone of the *second college in the English Colonies* was laid in 1695. Later this college was to stress secular as well as religious learning. The etiquette and manners of Southern society were emphasized. This college educated *Thomas Jefferson* and Chief Justice *John Marshall.* Its *School of Law* was the first of its kind in the Colonies.

3. **THE MIDDLE COLONIES.** Dutch and English attitudes affected education in the Middle Colonies of America. The Quakers had much influence. The following is an account of major events of the time in these colonies:

a. **New Jersey.** Because of troubled beginnings, the Colony of New Jersey did not have its own Governor until 1638. The English tradition of *little or no governmental interference* in education continued in this colony.

(1) **Act of 1693.** A law was promulgated in 1693 which *permitted towns to open their own schools.*

(2) **Act of 1695.** This act *turned all educational authority over to the individual towns.*

(3) **College of New Jersey.** A college was established at *Princeton* in 1746 to preserve the Puritan tradition. Under the impetus of Jonathan Edwards, new colleges were erected (Brown, Dartmouth, Princeton and Rutgers), during the revival of orthodox Calvinism. The College of New Jersey came to be called Princeton.

(4) **Queen's College.** The Scotch-Irish Presbyterians in 1756 opened Queen's College in New Jersey to train ministers. It became known as *Rutgers.*

b. **New York.** The Dutch placed education under the *control of the Church.* When the English took over in 1664, they left education without any governmental interference.

(1) **King's College.** King's College, founded in 1754, became known as *Columbia University.* Initially this college was *non-denominational.* It had a curriculum that was secular as well as religious.

c. <u>Pennsylvania.</u> The Quaker influence contributed to *the freedom of many religious beliefs* in this Colony. *Education was largely parochial.* The German Moravians established the first infant school. The Scotch-Irish Presbyterians opened the first grammar schools.

    (1) <u>The Philadelphia Academy.</u> Through the influence of Benjamin Franklin and the Junto philosophers, a secondary school was founded offering two courses of study, *Latin and English.* The English curriculum included the practical studies of *science, mathematics and navigation.* In 1755 the charter was rewritten to include the College, Academy and Charitable School of Philadelphia. This college later became known as the *University of Pennsylvania.* After 1755 the Latin and classical curriculum was offered only in the College. The Philadelphia Academy was the forerunner of many private academies which grew up in the next century and which continue to the present day.

EDUCATION DURING THE EARLY REPUBLIC OF THE UNITED STATES

EDUCATIONAL CHANGES. The following changes in the system of education in the United States took place after the founding of the Republic:

1. <u>RISE OF ACADEMIES.</u> The private academy became prominent on the American scene following the Revolution. *This academy became the foundation of American secondary education.* From about fifty schools in 1800, the academies numbered six thousand by the middle of the century. Eventually these academies moved away from practical education for living toward a curriculum which prepared students for college.

2. <u>FREE PUBLIC EDUCATION.</u> The *rise of industrialism,* requiring workers educated beyond rudimentary reading and writing, *the needs of democracy,* which meant new generations of educa ed free men were needed to continue the government of free men, and the *spirit of humanitarianism,* which desired the social lot of all men to be improved, led to the creation of a free public education. *The first free public high school appeared in Boston in 1821.* Through the efforts of Horace Mann, Massachusetts was the first state to move toward a free, public, non-sectarian school system.

3. <u>STATE SYSTEMS OF EDUCATION.</u> Because there was no mention of *education in the Constitution,* it was placed under the *control of each individual State.* This led to separate State systems of education, which accounts for the lack of uniformity in the growth of a free public education as well as agreement upon compulsory attendance laws.

4. <u>SPIRIT OF UTILITARIANISM.</u> The needs of frontier America led to an emphasis upon *practical subjects* in the curriculum. Latin and Greek, as well as classical literature, were replaced gradually with *mathematics, science, geography, economics and history.*

5. <u>COMPULSORY SCHOOL ATTENDANCE.</u> *The first law* compelling the attendance of every child between the ages of eight and fourteen was passed *in Massachusetts in 1852.* By 1918, compulsory education extended to every State. South Carolina, Mississippi and Virginia subsequently repealed their compulsory attendance laws.

6. <u>THE NORTHWEST ORDINANCE.</u> Sections of Federal land were given to towns for public education in 1787. In order to encourage free public education, Congress

granted *one-sixteenth of the land of each township* for the support of schools in the Ohio Territory. As each State entered the Union, it benefited by this law.

7. <u>LAND GRANT COLLEGES.</u> On July 2, 1862, Lincoln signed an act which made a *land grant of thirty thousand acres* for each Senator and Representative of every State in the Union *for the support of those colleges* whose major purposes were the teaching of *agriculture and the mechanical arts.*

8. <u>SUPREME COURT DECISIONS.</u> The Supreme Court protected the right of private education in the *Dartmouth Decision of 1819.* Chief Justice John Marshall declared that a college charter is a contract and therefore inviolable. The State is unable to take over a private institution. *The Kalamazoo Decision* in 1874 provided support for *school districts to collect taxes for the support of secondary school education.* This decision created the phenomenal growth of secondary education in the United States and signaled the beginning of the end for many private academies.

9. <u>TEACHER TRAINING.</u> The first school dedicated to the training of teachers began as the *State Normal School in Lexington, Massachusetts, in 1839.* These schools were organized through the influence of *Horace Mann.* Initially they were intended as a two-year course preparing women for elementary teaching. By 1920 these institutions were acceptable as institutions of higher education. The first national organization of teachers began in Philadelphia in 1857. This grew into the present *National Education Association.*

10. <u>SCHOOL ADMINISTRATION.</u> The first move toward a *State Superintendent* of schools was taken in *New York, in 1784,* with the acceptance of a Board of Regents of the University of the State of New York. By *1837,* the City of *Buffalo* initiated the office of *City Superintendent* of Schools. The United States Department of Education was created in 1867 to provide educational information and to improve school systems throughout the country. This department became the present *Office of Education.*

PROMINENT AMERICAN EDUCATORS OF THE NINETEENTH CENTURY

INTRODUCTION. The prominent American educators of the nineteenth century were Thomas Jefferson, Horace Mann and Henry Barnard.

EDUCATIONAL CONTRIBUTIONS OF THOMAS JEFFERSON. Jefferson made these contributions to education:

1. <u>FIRST PLAN FOR A STATE SYSTEM OF EDUCATION.</u> Jefferson presented in 1779 the following *plan to provide universal free education* in the State of Virginia:

    a. <u>County Elections.</u> *Three aldermen* would be elected in every county.
    b. <u>County Subdivision.</u> The aldermen would divide the county *into subdivisions of hundreds.*
    c. <u>Local Schools.</u> Children living in each subdivision *would attend school there.*
    d. <u>Number of Schools.</u> A school would have to be erected *in each subdivision.*
    e. <u>Expenses.</u> School expenses would have to be paid for by the *county taxes.*
    f. <u>Supervision.</u> A supervisor would be appointed for *every ten schools.*
    g. <u>Personnel.</u> The *supervisor would hire* the necessary teachers.
    h. <u>Curriculum.</u> The curriculum would include the basic elementary subjects of *reading, writing and arithmetic,* and also instruction in *Greek, Roman, English and American History.*
    i. <u>Free Tuition.</u> The child would have the *first three years* of tuition free.

    j. **Grammar Schools.** One grammar school would be built *for every twenty districts* and located in a central position.

    k. **Grammar School Funds.** This school would be supported by public funds.

    l. **Grammar School Curriculum.** The curriculum would include *Latin, Greek, English grammar, geography and higher mathematics.*

    m. **Supervision.** A member from each county would be on *a Board of Visitors* to supervise the grammar schools.

    n. **Scholarship.** *Each superintendent would recommend a poor boy* for a scholarship to the grammar school and thence on to William and Mary College at public expense.

    o. **Secularization.** *Jefferson recommended* secularizing the curriculum of William and Mary College.

2. **PHILOSOPHY OF EDUCATION.** Jefferson viewed education in a practical way:

    a. **A Necessity.** He felt education was a necessity for *the continuance of a free society.*

    b. **Mass Education.** It helped create an *informed citizenry* for the election and operation of government.

    c. **Opportunity.** Education developed a *natural aristocracy* of ability rather than of birth.

EDUCATIONAL CONTRIBUTIONS OF HORACE MANN. Perhaps no one more deserves the title of *father of American public school education* than Horace Mann. This list contains many of his *contributions to education and events in his life:*

1. **EARLY YOUTH.** Horace Mann was *born in Franklin, Massachusetts, May 4, 1796.* His youth was lived in poverty and hardship on the family farm. His schooling was limited to about three months of instruction during each year. However, he mastered the tenets of the orthodox Calvinist faith by the age of ten. He rejected this faith when he was twenty-three years old in favor of *Unitarianism.* His remarks to the graduating class at Antioch College a few weeks before his death, *"Be ashamed to die before you have won some battle for humanity,"* reflects his Unitarian convictions. These beliefs, accepting the possibility of improvement of the human race, played no small role in Mann's efforts to establish free, public, non-sectarian education for every man and woman.

2. **BROWN UNIVERSITY.** After receiving some private tutoring, Mann qualified for the sophomore class at Brown. When he graduated, he *studied law* and was admitted to the Bar in 1823.

3. **POLITICIAN.** Between 1827 and 1848, Horace Mann had a brilliant career, first as a *State Representative* and then as *a Senator,* in the Massachusetts Legislature. He was active in establishing a state mental hospital in Worcester, Massachusetts.

4. **SECRETARY OF THE MASS. STATE BOARD OF EDUCATION.** In 1837 Horace Mann accepted the position of *First Secretary of the State Board of Education* in Massachusetts. His humanitarian impulses led him to abandon a highly promising career in politics in favor of education. He took office at a time when glaring weaknesses existed in public education in Massachusetts. Mann achieved the following in his twelve years as First Secretary:

    a. **Campaigned for Education.** Realizing the need for public *support* and public *awareness* of the educational problems of poor teaching, substandard materials, inferior school committees and pupil absences, Mann campaigned throughout the State. This campaign was eminently successful. The *schools were improved everywhere in the State.*

b. **Established Schools For Teacher Training.** The first *Normal School for Teachers* was established in Lexington, Massachusetts, in 1839 through the efforts of Mann.

c. **Established School District Libraries.** Horace Mann improved education by advocating successfully the establishment of *free libraries.*

d. **Won Financial Backing for Public Education.** Mann knew the importance of money in making educational progress. Through his efforts, the wages of teachers were more than doubled, supervision of teaching improved with compensated school committees, fifty new secondary schools were built, State aid to education doubled, and textbooks and educational equipment improved.

e. **Extended His Influence Beyond Massachusetts.** Horace Mann edited the "*Common School Journal*" and wrote *twelve Annual Reports* which became famous. Some important Annual Reports were:

(1) **Fifth Annual Report (1841).** Mann argued successfully that *economic wealth would increase through an educated public.* It was therefore in the self-interest of business to pay the taxation for public education.

(2) **Seventh Annual Report (1843).** Horace Mann inspected and appraised favorably *the Prussian school system.* This report led to widespread improvement of education through the educational theories of Pestalozzi, Herbart and eventually Froebel.

(3) **Tenth Annual Report (1846).** Mann asserted that education was *a natural right* for every child. It is a necessary responsibility of the State to *insure that education was provided* for every child. This report led to the adoption of the *first State law requiring compulsory attendance* in school in 1852.

(4) **Twelfth Annual Report (1848).** He presented a rationale for the support of public education through *taxation.* Society improves as a result of an educated public. He argued for *non-sectarian* schools, so the taxpayer would not be in the position of supporting any established religion with which he might disagree in conscience.

5. **LAST YEARS.** Horace Mann resigned in 1848 to take a seat vacated in the *United States Congress.* In 1853 he assumed the *Presidency of Antioch College* in Yellow Springs, Ohio. He became President to implement his educational ideas in higher education. This college was coeducational and non-sectarian. The labor of raising funds for Antioch College weakened his health. *He died August 2, 1859.*

EDUCATIONAL CONTRIBUTIONS OF HENRY BARNARD (1811-1900). Henry Barnard with Horace Mann *contributed to the "great awakening" of the American public* to the necessity of free public education. His important contributions to education and events in his life follow:

1. **LIFE.** Barnard was *educated at Yale, studied law and served in the General Assembly of Connecticut.* In 1838 he helped the passage of a law to establish a *State Board of Commissioners for Common Schools* in Connecticut similar to the State Board in Massachusetts. Barnard became the first secretary for this board. Although the board lasted only four years, it achieved educational reforms in Connecticut similar to those in Massachusetts. *Barnard's efforts during this period achieved:*

  a. **State System.** The foundation of a *state system of education was due to his efforts.*

  b. **Finance.** He increased *financial backing* of public schools.

  c. **In the Schools.** Barnard improved *instruction and school facilities.*

2. **EDUCATIONAL POSITIONS.** Barnard became the Commissioner of Education in *Rhode Island* in 1843, Chancellor of the *University of Wisconsin* in 1858, President of *St. John's College* in 1866 and *the first United States Comissioner of Education* in 1867.

3. **WRITINGS.** Barnard established the *Connecticut Common School Journal* and the important *American Journal of Education.*

4. **THEORY.** Barnard believed intensely that education is the means for *social peace and progress.* The free public education of every child is a necessity for the continuance of *social order. The influence of education is eternal.* Therefore, good teaching, good teachers and good schools are vital concerns of every citizen.

JOHN DEWEY AND THE TWENTIETH CENTURY

INTRODUCTION. John Dewey is recognized as one of the great figures in educational history. His influence upon American education has been prodigious. The following are the chief events of his *life:*

1. **EARLY YOUTH.** John Dewey was *born in Burlington, Vermont, October 20, 1859.* He was educated in Vermont, graduating in 1879 from the University of Vermont. He taught school in Pennsylvania for two years. An article in the *Journal of Speculative Philosophy* in April, 1882, entitled "The Metaphysical Assumptions of Materialism" won favorable response. He entered *Johns Hopkins University* in 1882 as a graduate philosophy student. He emerged two years later as a doctor of philosophy.

2. **TEACHING CAREER.** One of Dewey's philosophy professors at Johns Hopkins Univeristy was appointed Chairman of Philosophy at the University of Michigan. Upon graduation Dewey was offered a position as Instructor of Philosophy there. Dewey taught at *Michigan between 1884 and 1888.* He taught for one year at the *University of Minnesota.* The Chairman of Philosophy died at the University of Michigan. John Dewey *returned to Michigan* as Professor and Chairman of the Department of Philosophy. In *1894* Dewey moved to *the University of Chicago* as Professor of Philosophy and Pedagogy. He began a *Laboratory School* at Chicago for the education of future teachers. This school applied the latest psychological findings, the newest methods and educational theory in the 'assroom. Future teachers could observe and become experienced in applying the best teaching techniques to the pupils of the Laboratory School. Between 1902 and 1904 Dewey was the Director of the School of Education and organizer of the Laboratory School at the University of Chicago. During this period he was associated with Hull House as well. In *1904* Dewey moved to *Columbia University.* He remained at Columbia as a professor of philosophy and professor at Teachers' College until his *retirement in 1931.*

3. **RETIREMENT.** Dewey was a Professor Emeritus of Philosophy in Residence at Columbia between 1930 and 1939. Although retired, Dewey was continually active in the social affairs of the day. He lectured for two years in China to future teachers. In 1937 he was the *chairman of the Commission of Inquiry* into the charges against Leon Trotsky brought by the Russian government. Dewey *helped establish* the *New School of Social Research* in New York City. He was active in beginning

a *teachers' union*. John Dewey added to his many writings additional works until *his death on June 1, 1952,* at the age of ninety-two.

THE MAJOR WRITINGS OF JOHN DEWEY. The following list includes many important works written by John Dewey:

1. MY PEDAGOGIC CREED. New York, E. K. Kellog and Co., 1897.
2. INTERPRETATION OF THE CULTURE-EPOCH THEORY. National Herbart Society Yearbook, 1896.
3. PSYCHOLOGY AND PHILOSOPHIC METHOD. Berkeley, University of Cal. Press, 1899.
4. THE SCHOOL AND SOCIETY. Univ. of Chicago Press, 1900 (revised 1915).
5. STUDIES IN LOGICAL THEORY. Univ. of Chicago Press, 1903.
6. LOGICAL CONDITIONS OF A SCIENTIFIC TREATMENT OF MORALITY. Univ. of Chicago Press, 1903.
7. ETHICS. New York, Henry Holt and Co., 1908.
8. THE INFLUENCE OF DARWIN ON PHILOSOPHY AND OTHER ESSAYS IN CONTEMPORARY THOUGHT. New York, Henry Holt and Co., 1910.
9. HOW WE THINK. New York, Heath and Co., 1910.
10. DEMOCRACY AND EDUCATION. New York, Macmillan, 1916.
11. ESSAYS IN EXPERIMENTAL LOGIC. Univ. of Chicago Press, 1916.
12. RECONSTRUCTION IN PHILOSOPHY. New York, Holt and Co., 1920.
13. HUMAN NATURE AND CONDUCT. New York, Holt and Co., 1922.
14. EXPERIENCE AND NATURE. Chicago, Open Court, 1925.
15. THE PUBLIC AND ITS PROBLEMS. New York, Holt and Co., 1927.
16. THE QUEST FOR CERTAINTY. New York, Minton, Balch and Co., 1929.
17. PHILOSOPHY AND CIVILIZATION. New York, Minton, Balch and Co., 1931.
18. ART AS EXPERIENCE. New York, Minton, Balch and Co., 1934.
19. A COMMON FAITH. Yale Univ. Press, 1934.
20. LIBERALISM AND SOCIAL ACTION. New York, Putnam, 1935.
21. EXPERIENCE AND EDUCATION. New York, Macmillan, 1938.
22. FREEDOM AND CULTURE. New York, Putnam, 1939.
23. PROBLEMS OF MEN. New York, Philosophical Library, 1946.
24. LOGIC, THE THEORY OF INQUIRY. New York, Holt and Co., 1938.

PHILOSOPHICAL AND EDUCATIONAL THEORY. Some important concepts in *the philosophy of John Dewey* are the following:

1. INSTRUMENTALISM. Dewey was influenced by the theory of evolution. He affirmed that *the mind* as well as the body *evolved. Ideas arise from experience* and are nothing more than *plans of action* by which the organism adjusts satisfactorily to his environment. *Thinking is the process* by which man adjusts. Thinking begins as a result of the *felt need* of the individual. All thinking is *problem centered.* The product of human thought is the instrument of action. *Human thinking is social* in that it occurs in a social milieu. *Social utility* is the test by which truth is established.

2. METHOD OF SCIENCE. The truths of philosophy are not privileged. If the scientist must subject his hypothesis to the careful scrutiny of controlled observations and verification, so must the philosopher. Through inquiry, collecting facts, experimentation and verification will the philosopher provide new truths. *The philosophical area of metaphysics is consequently meaningless* because the problems do not lend themselves to this kind of scrutiny.

3. **DEMOCRACY.** The best form of government is democratic government. The cornerstone of Dewey's thought is *growth*. *What contributes to individual and social growth is good.* In fact, the value of education exists to the extent it creates a desire for continued growth. A man is good to the extent that he is growing or becoming more good. Now, in a democracy the free interchange between men permits modification, change and growth. It is therefore the best form of government.

4. **THE SCHOOL.** The school is a miniature community. It provides for social and individual growth. He rejected the teaching of subjects for their own sake. Any subject is merely *a means* and *not a end in itself.* It is the *means* by which the individual *reconstructs his experience*, extracts its meaning and thereby prepares himself for the future. Even freedom is itself a means. The only freedom with enduring importance is the *intellectual freedom* of observation and judgment exercised for an intrinsically worthy end or purpose. *Education is a reorganization of experience which adds meaning and ability in the directing of subsequent experience.* The subject matter of the school should consist of *facts* which are observed, remembered, read, discussed and suggested for the purpose of solving some *felt problem.* Interest and motivation are essential elements in the learning process.

5. **THE NATURE OF EXPERIENCE.** Activity by itself never constitutes experience. The concept of experience involves the aspects of *doing and undergoing.* When the individual experiences something, he both acts upon it and enjoys or undergoes the consequences of it. *The connection between these active and passive elements* in experience is the measure of the experiential value.

6. **INFORMATION AND KNOWLEDGE.** Dewey deplored the rigid, passive and unquestioning methods of the traditional schools. Lectures merely provide the individual with information. The pupil must act upon the information through experience prior to the acquisition of knowledge.

7. **DISCIPLINE.** Discipline is internal and positive. A pupil must be trained to *consider his actions* so that he will undertake them with *deliberation.* A pupil is disciplined when he understands what he must do and is moved to undertake the action quickly, using the requisite means necessary. When the pupil possesses the power to *endure* in an intelligently induced course of action in the face of obstacles, he is disciplined.

8. **INDIVIDUAL DIFFERENCES.** Children must never be treated exactly alike. Each child has *needs and experiences which are uniquely his own.* The child should be interested in and disciplined toward the *development and maintenance of intelligence on an individual basis.* Since society changes, the individual pupil must *learn how to think* in order to cope with a *changing environment.* When a school achieves this with every child, the school *no longer merely perpetuates society.* It becomes an essential force in the reconstruction of society.

EDUCATIONAL CHANGES DURING THE TWENTIETH CENTURY. The following is a summary of major events in and contributions to *current educational practice:*

1. **EDUCATIONAL PHILOSOPHY.** The philosophy of John Dewey has been of great importance to thought about educational aims in America. Dewey influenced such educational theorists as *Kilpatrick, Bode and Brameld.* Some important statements of educational aims in our century were:

   a. **The Commission On Reorganization of Secondary Education (1918).** This commission listed the following *"cardinal principles of education":*

(1) Health
(2) Command of the Fundamental Processes
(3) Citizenship
(4) Vocation
(5) Worthy Home Membership
(6) Worthy Use of Leisure Time
(7) Ethical Character.

b. **The Educational Policies Commission of the N.E.A. (1938).** The N.E.A. commission provided an exhaustive list of *current school objectives.* These were the following:

(1) **Self-Realization.** The purpose of education is to produce a man with an inquiring mind, skilled in listening and communicating in his native language, solving problems, living a healthy life with social responsibility, thinking rationally and appreciating aesthetic beauty.

(2) **Human Relationship.** The educated person must be able to hold social interests first, live and enjoy human relationships, establish and maintain a democratic family life.

(3) **Economic Efficiency.** The school should produce an individual who selects his own vocation, understands and lives according to the requirements of his job, improves his working efficiency and plans his own economic life.

(4) **Civic Responsibility.** The school should aim at producing citizens loyal to the democratic ideal. Such persons would participate in civic responsibilities, respect the social rights of others, be sensitive to social problems and work to improve society.

2. **EDUCATIONAL PSYCHOLOGY.** During this century great strides have been made in the realm of psychology. The findings of such men as *Thorndike, Guthrie, Hull, Lewin, Koffka, and Skinner* contributed to educational theories on learning and personality. Building upon the monumental genius of *Sigmund Freud,* Neo-Freudians contributed understandings applicable to the mental health of teachers and pupils alike.

3. **EXPERIMENTS IN EDUCATION.** The famous *Eight Year Study,* which was carried on by the Progressive Education Association between the years of 1932 and 1940, examined the college progress of students from thirty experimental schools in order *to discover the effectiveness of progressive approaches in education* upon subsequent college work. The study reported that students from progressive schools achieved higher college grades, possessed effective study habits and were better adjusted socially than the high school graduates from traditional schools. These *progressive schools* stressed the following:

a. **Curriculum.** The curriculum was organized around *problems* affecting the *needs* of youth.

b. **Purpose and Methods.** School purpose and methods were aimed at the whole child—his emotional, physical and mental health, social and intellectual development.

GENERAL CHARACTERISTICS OF TWENTIETH-CENTURY AMERICAN EDUCATION.

INTRODUCTION. Current policy and practice in the United States regarding education is dealt with in these eight points:

1. UNIVERSAL EDUCATION FOR ALL. During the first forty years of this century, the number of *high school graduates doubled each decade*. Following the second World War, this number increased because of the population explosion and *job requirements* in an increasingly technical and automated society. Programs such as *"Head Start"* provide a *nursery school education* for children in culturally deprived areas. *The Community College movement* adds millions of students more to higher education. State Colleges and Universities offer low-cost tuition rates for qualified students.

2. TEACHER CERTIFICATION AND EDUCATION. Although some school districts continue the practice of employing unqualified teachers, the majority of school systems *select teachers certified by the State Boards of Education*. These teachers are *educated better* than a century ago. Some think that teacher education will improve in quality still further, when the influence of extreme progressivists is limited in the Teacher Colleges.

3. CURRICULUM VARIETY. As the schools grow larger, accommodating children from a variety of localities, *the course of studies varies with the needs of the individual pupil*. Vocational studies, home economics, business, art and physical education are given along with the traditional subjects of languages, social studies, science, mathematics and civics. The grouping of students is based upon individual needs, interests and abilities. These are determined by carefully-prepared testing programs, utilizing intelligence and achievement tests.

4. METHODOLOGY. One of the most significant changes has taken place in classroom practices. Due to the influence of *psychological knowledge*, textbooks are no longer dull. *Books are colorful* and attractive. Pictures, charts and diagrams are scattered plentifully through the pages of textbooks. Classroom activities afford more mobility and added experience to pupils. There exists a greater reliance upon *audio-visual aids, field trips and projects*. There is less dependence upon recitation and lecture.

5. TEACHER-PUPIL RELATIONS. Today students and teachers seem to be *more active and more informal* in their relationships than ever before. The teacher accepts the fact that he is responsible for the emotional and social development of the child, as well as his intellectual growth.

6. SCHOOL ORGANIZATION. The usual organization of the school system provides for a *six-year elementary school, a three-year junior high school and a three-year senior high school*. This system provides for the special needs of the early adolescent. It enables the school to organize the curriculum in such a way as to provide the early adolescent with exploratory experiences in a variety of vocational areas.

7. SCHOOL ADMINISTRATION. The large numbers of pupils, teachers, and schools have given rise to *specialization in administration as a separate professional function*. Most States require school principals and superintendents to have special course preparations in schools of education before certification. Courses in administration, curriculum, supervision, finance and school law prepare future school administrators.

8. NON-DENOMINATIONAL. The struggle to keep the public schools free of sectarian bias resulted in the famous *school-prayer decision of the Supreme Court in 1962*. The Court ruled that the Regents of the State of New York acted unconstitutionally

in recommending the recitation of the State-written school prayer. Horace Mann was successful in keeping public education separate from religious groups. In 1925, almost a hundred years after the beginning of public education, the Supreme Court ruled in favor of the existence of private religious education in an Oregon decision. Those who believed that religion was inseparable from the educational processes were free to send their children to *private parochial schools*. The public schools however have been protected consistently by the Supreme Court from the domination of any one religion. Although the Court supported released time for religious education in the 1952 Zorach decision, this education could not take place on school property according to the McCollum decision of 1948. Finally the *Schemp decision of 1963* outlawed all Bible reading and prayers.

EDUCATION AND WORLD SURVIVAL

INTRODUCTION. The twentieth century has been confronted with a deep economic depression, two world wars and a number of minor conflicts. In order to adapt education to the needs of a world constantly facing disaster, *two educational positions emerged*. These positions became clear following the controversy between *the "progressivists" and the "essentialists"* at a meeting of the American Association of School Administrators in Atlantic City in 1938.

PROGRESSIVISM

BEGINNINGS. The *Progressive Education Association* began in the United States in *1918. William Heard Kilpatrick* was one of the foremost spokesmen for Progressives in the United States.

PROGRESSIVE AIM. Motivated by the threats of totalitarianism and economic depression, the Progressives attempted to maintain a position between the extremes of static objectives based upon an ideal society and the individualism that asserted that the only goal is the individual growth of the child. The progressivist aim is:

1. **PERSONALITY GROWTH THROUGH SOCIAL COOPERATION.** The pupil interacts with his environment. As he improves, he affects his surroundings in a favorable manner. *Education must aim at the improvement of every individual* in order to have a better democratic society. Plato had taught that justice could never exist upon an individual basis. He thought that one required a utopian just state in order to have individual morality. Progressives take the opposite position. *Social improvement begins with the individual who is free to grow in a democratic society*.

PROGRESSIVE EDUCATION. Since education is a matter of interaction between the individual and his society or environment, *the whole child* must be provided with *every kind of experience* found in his culture that will produce growth. The educational principles are:

1. **THE CHILD LEARNS AS A WHOLE.** The school must not ignore the emotions of the child in learning. These emotions are not separate from the intellectual development of the child. (This position is contrary to the position of Piaget in learning theory. However, Piaget's assertions are unverified). The schools therefore ought not to educate the mental, emotional and physical aspects of the child as separate entities.

2. CURRICULUM. The school must repudiate the subject-centered curriculum. It must provide the pupil with *all the experiences possible* that will permit him to interact with his environment. The curriculum is an experience centered, activity type of curriculum. Progressivists believe that learning occurs:

a. <u>Learning.</u> Learning occurs through the *personal experience* of the *total organism*. This experience allows the child to:

    (1) <u>Expand.</u> The pupil acquires a variety of experiences from his environment.
    (2) <u>Differentiation.</u> The pupil selects those experiences which he judges valuable for his purposes.
    (3) <u>Integration.</u> The pupil makes the meaningful experience a part of himself.

b. <u>Through a Holistic Type of Curriculum.</u> The pupil learns best in *a curriculum organized along broad general lines.* A core of experiences necessary for the social development of every citizen should be provided by the school. The pupil would subsequently be free to pursue his own intellectual interests following the common studies. *Continuity* in the curriculum is provided by *the relevancy* of material *integrated by* the individual.

ESSENTIALISM

INTRODUCTION. The Essentialist tradition is a long one in the history of education. It numbers among its members the Aristotelians, and the seventeenth century realists such as Bacon, Locke, Comenius, Ratke and Francke. William Chandler Bagley and Frederick S. Breed were the chief advocates for Essentialism in the United States during the early debates between Progressives and Essentialists.

ESSENTIALIST AIMS. Motivated by the threat to democratic society, the Essentialists asserted that education must serve the preservation of democracy. They believed that *Progressivism leads* to the development of *undisciplined, uneducated and immature citizens* who will be unable to preserve the democratic way of life. Education ought to do the following:

1. <u>PREPARE THE CHILD WITH THOSE COMPETENCIES NECESSARY FOR A SATISFACTORY ADJUSTMENT TO THE REAL WORLD.</u> The essential knowledge, skills, attitudes and appreciations have not been acquired by accident. *The immature child depends upon adult instruction* in the common objectives of humanity. The goals of the school cannot be separate from the democratic values of the society in which it exists. The school ought to provide the essential competencies to preserve the democratic society. *The child is dependent upon adult instruction* to provide him with those competencies which are necessary for him to adjust to the moral, intellectual and vocational demands of a responsible adult life.

ESSENTIALIST EDUCATION. The ultimate purpose of education is *the development of a self-direction* in the child which will enable him to *intelligently and freely* choose those actions which will preserve our democratic society. The school should provide him with the competencies and guidance to do this. The educational principles are:

1. <u>INTEREST AND MOTIVATION.</u> It is true that motivation is vital to learning. How-

ever, it is the duty of the teacher to assist the child *to rise above his level of interest* and acquire an interest in the less-appealing intellectual competencies.

2. <u>DISCIPLINE.</u> Freedom by itself may lead to chaos and social anarchy. The pupil ought to be habituated into choosing socially desirable actions. The school *must retain a disciplinary guidance* to inhibit undesirable actions.

3. <u>THINKING.</u> The child must develop skill in thinking. *Thinking* does not develop in a haphazard fashion. It *is systematic.* The pupil cannot develop these skills by looking at the broad range of knowledge. *He should be provided with:*

    a. <u>Essential Knowledge.</u> Knowledge recognized by humanity as necessary for certain truths is a prerequisite.

    b. <u>Practice.</u> Practice is needed in using this knowledge to solve real problems.

    c. <u>Guidance.</u> There can be a guidance of free decisions arrived at by the pupil.

4. <u>CURRICULUM.</u> The Essentialist recommends a subject matter curriculum which *systematically transmits* the essential elements of human culture. The psychological principles of learning ought to relate to the *logical organization* and sequence of the essential subjects.

14 | WORLD EDUCATION TODAY

INTRODUCTION. What schools ought to do has been resolved by different societies throughout the history of education according to the nature of each society. In general, the *schools have served a practical purpose*. They provided the society with the means for its survival. However *certain conflicts* exist, such as:

1. **SOCIAL OR INDIVIDUALISTIC.** Education should exist primarily for the individual *or* it should exist primarily for the preservation of society.
2. **CONFORMITY OR CREATIVE EXPRESSION.** Education should stress the acquisition of social values *or* it should encourage original thinking about changing societies.
3. **STATE OR FAMILY.** Education should be the primary responsibility of the state *or* it should be the chief concern of the family.
4. **PRACTICAL OR INTELLECTUAL.** Education should aim at developing useful abilities and skills *or* education ought to emphasize intellectual growth and erudition.
5. **LIMITED OR UNIVERSAL.** Education should be the prerogative of the few who are capable of higher learning *or* it ought to include all men and women in the society.

EDUCATION TODAY IN THE ORIENT

CHINA. Following World War II, a devastated China faced the horror of another war. This civil war resulted in a Communist victory. The educational system has been built along the Marxist principles evident in Russian education. There is a move toward these policies:

1. **UNIVERSAL EDUCATION.** Everybody has a right to be educated.
2. **GOVERNMENT.** The government has introduced control, supervision and indoctrination.
3. **EARLY TRAINING.** Children are taken at the earliest age possible and subjected to an intense program of Communist indoctrination.

JAPAN. General McArthur, during the American occupation, attempted to move Japan toward democracy. The schools were a principal means for achieving this goal. The *education of Japan* is characterized by:

1. **AMERICAN SCHOOL ORGANIZATION.** There exists a six-year elementary school, a three-year junior high school and a three-year senior high school. College courses last four years.
2. **EQUAL EDUCATIONAL OPPORTUNITY FOR ALL.** Girls were allowed educational rights for the first time in Japanese history. Today there are as many girls as boys in school beyond the age of compulsory attendance.
3. **COMPULSORY EDUCATION.** All children are required to attend school until the

113

age of fifteen. Sixty-two per cent of the children who finish junior high school go on to senior high school, as of 1962.

4. <u>STATE ASSISTANCE.</u> The government has provided free textbooks for all elementary school children since 1963. The pupils are required to pay a $10 tuition fee in secondary senior high schools. Children in private schools pay as much as $104 per year. Those pupils unable to pay any tuition may attend school on a part-time basis.
5. <u>HIGHER EDUCATION.</u> The cost of higher education is a serious problem in contemporary Japan. Faculty salaries are very low. There are not enough funds to provide a sufficient number of scholarships or to erect buildings to house the growing demand for college education.

INDIA. Education in India has been handicapped by:

1. <u>POVERTY.</u> Although the individual States have controlled education since 1921, all of them are dependent upon the Central Government for *financial support*. In an overpopulated country where starvation is not uncommon, the financing of education is a serious problem.
2. <u>INEQUALITY.</u> India is a country of extremes in wealth and poverty. The *caste system* remains under the surface as an obstacle to equal opportunity.
3. <u>ENGLISH OCCUPATION.</u> Although India is now a free and independent member of the British Commonwealth, Indian secondary education labors under the handicap of British education. *Mahatma Gandi* at *Wardha* in *1937*, recommended a new type of basic education that would stress the development of the whole child through crafts, skills and related subjects. He also wanted the official language of India, Hindi, to replace English in secondary schools.

BASIC EDUCATION IN INDIA. One of the primary goals of Indian education was to make the educational system *consistent with Indian rather than Western culture*. Article 45 of the Indian Constitution placed responsibility upon the States of India to provide compulsory education for every child between six and fourteen. By 1962 about sixty-six per cent of the school-aged children were in school until eleven years old. Twenty-seven per cent of the children attended school between the ages of eleven and fourteen. *Basic education* is divided into:

1. <u>PRIMARY SCHOOL.</u> This school is for children between the ages of six and eleven. The curriculum develops skills in *vocational crafts, math and science, social studies and the study of the vernacular language.*
2. <u>MIDDLE SCHOOL.</u> This school is for children between the ages of eleven and fourteen. In some states these schools are *extended three years* to provide a terminal education for students.
3. <u>VOCATIONAL SCHOOL.</u> This school is a *six-year* school. Pupils may enter directly from primary school or three years later from the middle school.
4. <u>SECONDARY SCHOOL.</u> This school prepares pupils for university. Although there is a movement to create large multi-purpose secondary schools, few of these schools exist. The majority of the secondary schools are run in English *along the traditional lines of the English public school.*

EDUCATION TODAY IN THE MAJOR POWERS OF EUROPE

ENGLAND. Education in England was controlled largely by the Church of England from the Reformation to the late nineteenth century. The following developments then took place:

1. **ELEMENTARY EDUCATION ACT of 1870.** This Act authorized the *levying of local taxes to support free public elementary education*. These taxes could also be used to support the elementary Church schools. The public schools were operated by elected school boards. Hence the name "boardster" school was used to describe them.
2. **EDUCATION ACT of 1902.** This Act authorized taxation to establish and *support a free secondary school* in each county.
3. **THE FISHER ACT of 1918.** This Act authorized the establishment and support of public nursery schools. It provided in addition a number of scholarships to encourage attendance in secondary schools by poor children.
4. **THE EDUCATION ACT of 1944.** This act *made education compulsory* for all children between five and fifteen. It aimed at extending free public education for all for as long as possible in a unified system of education.

PUBLIC ELEMENTARY EDUCATION. In England the *elementary school is divided into:*

1. **NURSERY SCHOOL.** This is a voluntary school for children aged two to five.
2. **INFANT SCHOOL.** The child begins this school at the age of five. Education is compulsory at this level for those children who do not have private tutors.
3. **JUNIOR SCHOOL.** A school which takes children between the ages of eight and eleven.

SECONDARY EDUCATION. When the child is eleven, he may take an examination to determine the type of secondary education he will undertake. The types of secondary education are:

1. **VOCATIONAL SCHOOL.** This is a three-year school which prepares the pupil in some technical skill.
2. **COMPREHENSIVE HIGH SCHOOL.** This school offers a variety of subjects. Usually pupils in this school *do not continue on into college*. Some do continue their education further.
3. **GRAMMAR SCHOOL.** The free grammar school prepares pupils of ages twelve to seventeen for college entrance. There are private preparatory schools, which are called public schools in England, that perform the same function.
4. **SECONDARY MODERN SCHOOL.** This school is a three-year school for pupils who terminate their education at fifteen.

HIGHER EDUCATION. There exists both public and private colleges in England. Higher education includes technical colleges and colleges of teacher training.

SCOTLAND AND NORTHERN IRELAND. The Education Act of 1945 in Scotland and the Education Act of 1947 in Northern Ireland extended the provisions of the English Act of 1944. These *three acts provided for universal opportunity* in education throughout Great Britain. While religious and private schools are protected in their existence, non-denominational public instruction is available in an organized and supervised system.

GERMANY. After World War II, Germany was divided into four zones of occupation. In 1939 there were 1,558 school buildings. After the war only 162 of these buildings remained. The allies abolished the Reich Ministry of Education and the Prussian Ministry of Education in an effort to re-educate Germany. The aggressive nationalism and Naziism had to be eliminated from the social scene. The *British and American zones* placed the responsibility for education in local civilian hands. The *Russian and French zones* held tight control over every educational activity. *Little was a-chieved toward universal free education prior to 1949.*

WEST GERMANY. The Federal Republic of Germany defines itself as a democratic state with all ultimate authority vested in the people. This West German Republic was brought into existence on September 21, 1949. It consists of ten states with separate state governments. *Education is controlled on the state level.* The chief school officer for each state is a member of the *Permanent Conference of Ministers of Education* (established in 1948), who resolves common national problems. The executive secretary of the Conference is a member of the Permanent Conference of Ministers under the Ministry of the Interior.

EDUCATIONAL PRACTICE. German education varies with the individual states in West Germany. In general, free and universal education is compulsory for all children between six and fourteen. (Three states extend compulsory education to fifteen years of age). All children must attend the *basic elementary school* (Volksschule) for *four years.* Some continue in the basic school for another four years. Some transfer to the *middle school* (Mittelschule) for another *three to six years.* And others enter the *secondary schools.* There is a variety of secondary schools. Many of these schools stress social studies to a degree never before known in German education.

EAST GERMANY. In 1952 the state system was abolished in East Germany. There are *fifteen administrative units* responsible to *one central authority.* The educational system is similarly managed. Education in East Germany can be summarized in the following way:

1. <u>AIM.</u> The purpose of education is to develop a *patriotic* citizen who will serve Communist society.
2. <u>COMPULSORY EDUCATION.</u> This extends to all children in the new (1965) *ten-year school.* This school includes eight years of elementary education and two years of secondary education.
3. <u>FREE SCHOOLING.</u> Education and free texts are provided at every level of education—elementary through college.
4. <u>HIGHER EDUCATION.</u> Those citizens who complete the *ten-year school* may attend a *technical college* or enroll in night adult school for further education. Students who complete the eight-year elementary and four-year secondary courses or the secondary education in the ten-year school with a certificate of maturity may enter a university.

FRANCE. The educational committee headed by Paul Langevin in 1947 recommended a type of education on two levels:

1. <u>PRIMARY DEGREE.</u> This includes all primary, intermediate and secondary education in every field—vocational or theoretical. This education would take in pupils between the ages of six and eighteen.
2. <u>SECONDARY DEGREE.</u> This level includes all higher education, both technical and academic.

EDUCATION DECREE OF 1959. This act created the General Directorate of School Organization and Curriculum. The Directorate is responsible for *coordinating all secondary education*. In France education is:

1. <u>COMPULSORY.</u> School is compulsory for all between the ages of six and fifteen.
2. <u>MODERN AND CLASSICAL LYCEES.</u> These are secondary schools that offer a variety of curricula suited to the individual's needs.
3. <u>TERMINAL EDUCATION.</u> Children who are not inclined toward higher education get *vocational training* in the final years following primary education.
4. <u>SECONDARY EXAMINATIONS.</u> The examinations following the completion of Lycee have been extended to include industrial and economic studies as well as the academic subjects.
5. <u>PRIVATE AND RELIGIOUS EDUCATION.</u> These exist alongside public education. In *1951* the French Government permitted the granting of *scholarships* to children attending Catholic schools. This aided the financially oppressed parochial system.

RUSSIA. Education in the Soviet Union is free and available to every citizen. Prior to the Communist revolution, Russia had the highest rate of illiteracy of any major civilized country. Today illiteracy is almost non-existent. Education holds a privileged position in Russian thought. Some important characteristics of education there are:

1. <u>COMPULSORY EDUCATION.</u> Every person must attend *seven grades of schooling*.
2. <u>FREE EDUCATION.</u> This exists on every level save in the nursery school. The parents of children in nursery school are required to pay tuition in accordance with their economic ability.
3. <u>THE AIM OF EDUCATION.</u> Schools exist to make men Communist-oriented citizens. A sense of responsibility to society and a materialistic view of the world are recommended. This indoctrination begins in the nursery school.
4. <u>TEN-YEAR SCHOOL.</u> This school includes primary and secondary education. The curriculum would be described in the United States as "essentialist." Science, math, foreign languages, the Russian language and literature, history, geography and physical education are emphasized. *Discipline, respect for authority* and *responsibility* are stressed throughout the pupil's schooling. Heavy homework, competition and examinations are common.
5. <u>HIGHER EDUCATION.</u> Opportunities of this exist for those who are able to pass the rigid requirements. Higher education is free. The students who excel are rewarded with additional financial assistance.

QUESTIONS AND ANSWERS

QUESTION 1.

What were the characteristics of education in ancient civilizations?

ANSWER.

Education was *controlled by the priests* in ancient civilizations, with the exception of China. Formal classes were held in areas adjacent to the temples. The curriculum as a result included religious dogma that tended to continue the religious mythology of the time. What education existed usually was reserved for the upper classes. Children from the working class were trained in the vocation of the father at home. Indian education influenced all of Asia. Persian influence upon our Western civilization was equally important. Having assimilated Egyptian learning, the Persians contributed through the Moslems to us a knowledge of mathematics, astronomy, medicine and literature. These subjects had their beginnings in ancient times.

QUESTION 2.

What are the values to be derived from a study of the history of education?

ANSWER.

The student who studies the history of education has an opportunity to understand the *aims, content, administration, methods and teaching* in every civilization from the beginning of recorded history until the present. This information provides him with opportunities to assess the strengths and weaknesses of educational systems with a view to understanding and improving the present educational system. It may be further understood that education is the single most important *social activity for the preservation of the state* outside of the family. The student is afforded the opportunity to evaluate the role of education in contributing to the success or weakness of the civilization. Knowledge about great thinkers and contributors to education down the centuries is enriching and useful in evaluating contemporary education.

QUESTION 3.

What were the differences between the curricula of Sparta and Athens? What was the reason for these differences?

ANSWER.

The education of the *Spartan* boy stressed only physical development and moral development. Girls were educated exclusively in gymnastics and domestic arts. This curriculum reflected the social aims of Spartan society. Sparta was populated by a conquering Spartan people who were outnumbered by the large mass of conquered Helots (original residents of the territory). In order to preserve the supremacy of the Spartan over the enslaved natives it became necessary for them to establish a military state. The Spartan boy had to be trained to become an outstanding warrior with all the important attributes of the successful military man. These included great patriotism, instant obedience to orders, physical strength and endurance, skill in arms, tactics and strategy, and courage and readiness to serve the state in time of need. It was believed that all girls should be provided with physical training so that their future children would be strong and healthy.

Girls *in Athens* were educated in the domestic arts at home. Boys received an education in the liberal arts. These subjects were expected to liberate the mind of the free man so that he might effectively live a leisured existence and contribute to the welfare of the democratic state by judicious voting. The curriculum consisted of *reading, writing, arithmetic and music at the elementary level.* The *secondary school offered grammar, rhetoric, geometry, art and music.* When higher education developed, *philosophy* was the major subject. Higher education included rhetoric, and some science and mathematics in later years. This education reflected a democratic society in which the menial tasks were performed by slaves. It was a society in which women were relegated to a relatively inferior status.

QUESTION 4.

Discuss Plato's theory of education.

ANSWER.

Plato described his ideal education in *The Republic.* He assumed that justice could exist only when there was *a just state* possessing the virtues of wisdom, courage and temperance. These separate virtues would derive from different groups of people — the philosopher-kings who would administer the state according to the dictates of wisdom, the warriors who would defend the state according to the virtue of courage and the peasants and workers who would provide the necessary food and services, living lives of temperance. The state would hold complete control over property, marriage, education and procreation. This communist state would provide for each individual's needs and receive from each individual whatever he was able to produce. With the elimination of wealth and family life (which tends to favor wealth by passing possessions on to children), the just state would have no internal conflicts between the haves and the have-nots.

Education is the means by which the just communist state continues. Children are obtained through selective breeding to improve the race. These children are taken by the state and raised and educated into a life of service to the state. *All rights belong to the state and never reside in the individual.* Each individual receives whatever he has through the state. Education should include both boys and girls. Whatever children exhibit an aptitude for higher learning should be provided with the opportunity of engaging in the lengthy education which leads to the administrative positions. Other children would be educated in military school or in vocational skills according to their abilities. All children would receive an elementary education including character development, physical development and music.

QUESTION 5.

What was the contribution of Aristotle to education?

ANSWER.

Aristotle was the first to suggest *that education is the responsibility of the state*. He thought that the state should provide each citizen with an education commensurate with his ability. An educated public would advance the welfare of the society in which it lived. Each government should have an educational system appropriate to the type of government that existed. Education must aim at developing *a sound body and a sound mind*. Good health is necessary for any of life's activities. However, the highest faculty of man is his reason. *It is his reason that makes man unique in the world*. The faculty of reason, proceeding from the passive and active soul, must be educated. Science and philosophy contribute to this development. When man is educated to his fullest potential, education has served its purpose. The development of vocational skills merely trains a man. True education relates to the means by which the potentialities inherent in human nature are developed. Education must concern itself with liberating the potential resident in the nature of every human being.

QUESTION 6.

Discuss the development of education in Rome.

ANSWER.

In the early days of the Roman Republic, the purpose of education was *the development of a strong character*, obedient to family and state. Education was a practical affair which took place in the home. *The plebeian child* received a moral education, first from his mother and then from some older female relative living in the house. Then he apprenticed himself to the trade of his father, learning from him whatever skills were necessary. The education of *the patrician child* followed a similar practical pattern. When the boy grew older he accompanied a relative into the Senate and observed the practical affairs of speaking and administering the government.

When Rome conquered Greece, the education of the Greeks became the major educational influence in Rome. *Greek slaves taught the children of Rome* as tutors and as instructors in the schools. It was recognized during the days of the emperors that a state system of organized education was necessary. This interest of the emperors in educational matters evolved slowly. Complete state control of education existed by the fourth century A.D.

QUESTION 7.

Describe the theory of Quintilian in education.

ANSWER.

Quintilian advanced *the first systematic statement* on the problems of education. The *Education of the Orator* represents his major work upon educational theory and methodology. Quintilian suggested that teachers be selected with great care. The vocation of teaching is too important to entrust it to inferior people. A public school education is far superior to a private education in which a child is trained by a tutor at home. The social intercourse provided by a public school, along with its carefully selected teachers, is of greater value. Teachers, he thought, must strive to *base the lessons upon the interests of the child.* He abhorred cruel physical punishment. Quintilian held that *punishment is a barrier to learning.* The teacher should be aware that each child is different and learns at a different pace. A child must never be punished for his inability to grasp a lesson.

QUESTION 8.

Discuss the attitude of early Christianity to education.

ANSWER.

The early Christians held that education must provide the human being with a knowledge of the doctrine and morals of Christianity. This knowledge ought to be accompanied by strength of character and the will to act virtuously in order to achieve *the eternal reward of an immortal life with God.* Whatever distracts the person from his eternal goal is evil. Thus the non-Christian theories of the ancient philosophers, the literature of paganism which extolled sensual pleasure and secular concern with earthly existence became anathema to the early Christian leaders. As a result many pagan works were destroyed by the Christians. Plato's works, however, survived because of the praise given him by such early Christian Fathers as St. Augustine. In order to protect their faith, schools which were exclusively Christian were established. The early *catechumen schools* were devoted to educating the convert in the truths of the faith. Many of their religious leaders were educated at these schools.

QUESTION 9.

Discuss the effect of the Christian doctrine of Original Sin upon later educational theory.

ANSWER.

It was asserted that the sin of Adam (the first man) brought upon his progeny a state of spiritual darkness in which man would be *inclined toward evil.* As such, man would certainly be condemned upon death to a life of eternal separation from God. However, the redemptive act of Christ, by which He died upon the cross, provides his faithful followers with eternal salvation. Yet the faithful follower must *ever be on guard against pernicious influence* which could incline him toward evil. Subsequent Christian thinkers, such as Calvin, stressed Original Sin to the extent that man's nature was declared totally depraved because of the event. Man therefore is evil in his every action.

Discipline was harsh in the Calvinist schools. The child was considered naturally bad. It was *the function of education to counter the evil inclinations of the child* with moral precepts and strict procedures. The early textbooks included constant admonitions and pious recommendations.

QUESTION 10.

Give an account of the development of Medieval education.

ANSWER.

When the Roman empire fell to the barbarian hordes that overran Europe, the only schools to survive were those *schools attached to the monasteries.* With the development and spread of monastacism throughout Western Europe in the early Middle Ages, the number of these monastic schools increased. Each school taught some few children the rudiments of reading and writing, along with large portions of Christian doctrine.

Another type of school was *the cathedral school.* Initially this school was intended as a school of music for future choir singers. The cathedral school became, along with the monastic school, the main source of secondary education during the Middle Ages.

Charlemagne provided great stimulus for education by enlivening the *Palace School* with the greatest teacher in Europe at the time, *Alcuin.* The legislation by which Charlemagne extended education throughout the Holy Roman Empire led to the extension and improvement of education.

The Moslem translations of the ancient philosophers and learned commentaries upon their works led to the stimulation of higher learning. *Schools of higher learning were communities of teachers and scholars gathered to study* and investigate some areas of common interest. Thus the University of Paris began as a school of theology, Bologna as a school of law and Salerno as a school of medicine. The greatest of the first medieval universities was the *University of Paris.* Oxford University in England began as an outgrowth of the Paris university. Cambridge University was established as an extension of Oxford.

QUESTION 11.

What is scholasticism?

ANSWER.

Scholasticism is a theologically framed system of philosophy. During the Middle Ages, Christian theologians worked to achieve *a synthesis of pagan Greek philosophy with Christian doctrine.* St. Thomas *Aquinas* was the greatest of these theologians. His system applied the philosophy of Aristotle in support of the theological dogmas of the Faith. His systematic presentation placed heavy reliance on the importance of *reason.* During the Reformation a conflict arose between *Luther* and Scholasticism upon the issue of reason. Luther preferred the Augustinian tradition which emphasized *the will* that is involved in the act of faith. Man is saved by faith alone according to Luther. Luther believed man is so depraved by Original Sin that his reason is not trustworthy. However, the scholastics used reason only to support what they already had accepted through faith.

QUESTION 12.

Why did Martin Luther urge universal education on the elementary level?

ANSWER.

Luther believed that *the Bible was the sole rule of faith*. An individual learned the moral precepts through reading the Bible. Under the guidance of the Holy Spirit the person could interpret the meaning of what was read in the Bible. Everyone therefore should possess the skill and understanding necessary for reading the Scriptures. Since church services included the collective singing of hymns, rudimentary knowledge of music was required.

QUESTION 13.

What did Martin Luther think of coeducation?

ANSWER.

Luther disapproved of anything but basic elementary education for girls. He considered *the place of a woman was in the home*. She should be trained in the domestic skills necessary in the operation of her future home. Secondary education and university education were for men only.

QUESTION 14.

Why did the Protestant reformers prefer public education?

ANSWER.

Education had been under the control of the Church prior to the Reformation. In revolting against Papal authority, it became important for the reformers to assert a political theory which would offer the secular authorities greater power in temporal and religious affairs. Luther viewed the function of *the secular prince as that of protector of religion*. It was the duty of the prince to correct the religious leaders when they strayed from the ancient Christian faith. This prince must insure the fact that his subjects are provided with the education necessary to carry on the functions of religion and the state. The public school therefore was a secular and a religious school. Because there existed no separation between the state and the approved church, the school which the state supported contained both elements — secular and religious. The authoritative position of the prince made education his responsibility.

QUESTION 15.

Why were the Jesuit schools excellent institutions of learning?

ANSWER.

When the Jesuits put their plan of studies into effect, their schools rapidly became among the best in Europe. An important factor in their educational success was the outstanding *quality of teachers* in their schools. The teacher was selected with great care. Only those who exhibited high intelligence, enthusiasm for teaching, love of youth and successful classroom teaching were acceptable as teachers. The Jesuit order was the first to demand the systematic training of teachers. Each of their teachers received careful training in pedagogy prior to teaching. The study of teaching methods, the period of practice teaching and the very careful supervision of new teachers contributed to their quality. The *teaching methods* were of equal importance. Jesuit teachers were expected to know each student, to stimulate interest in the lesson, to treat every student with fairness and to be a guide to him.

QUESTION 16.

What were the characteristics of English education at the time of the Reformation?

ANSWER.

Although some doctrinal dispute existed between the English Throne and the Papacy, the major source of disagreement derived from the clash for ecclesiastical control. Educational control as a result was left in the hands of the Anglican Church. *Anglican ecclesiastical authority controlled the license and certification of teachers and the curriculum* of the schools until the middle of the nineteenth century. This indifference of secular authority to education impeded the growth of free, universal public education in England. This in turn contributed to the exceptionally high illiteracy rate in England among the common people.

QUESTION 17.

Explain the importance of Comenius in the history of education.

ANSWER.

Comenius promoted an educational theory based upon *the nature and needs of children*. He held the curriculum ought to offer *vernacular studies* rather than emphasize the old classical languages. This content should be taught in an interesting way in order to arouse involvement in the lesson. To ensure the ready understanding of children, the teacher should arrange every lesson in such a way that the child may observe and become active in the learning situation. The lessons should be concrete and appeal to the senses of the child. It is through *the senses* that a child learns. Finally the school experience must be as pleasant as possible. Good buildings and pleasant surroundings contribute to the child's learning. Punishment should never be associated with schoolwork.

QUESTION 18.

Why is John Locke important to education?

ANSWER.

Locke's educational theory would not be completely acceptable to most Americans today. Locke advocated *quality education only for the aristocracy*. They would be the future leaders of the nation. *The common man required only vocational skill and social understanding.* Locke is of great importance, however, for his psychological insight into *the learning processes.* He also believed that one must be educated for the society in which one lived. Education must serve a useful purpose.

It was Locke's insistence upon *the sensory quality in learning* that stimulated future theorists to propose sound psychological procedures in teaching. He believed that the mind of man was blank at birth. Through sense experience, specific sensations were impressed on the brain. The association of these impressions led to the intellectual perception of new ideas. This psychological theory foreshadowed the work of *associationistic psychologists* centuries later.

QUESTION 19.

Discuss the educational importance of the novel *Emile.*

ANSWER.

Rousseau influenced many great figures in education through his novel, *Emile.* Basedow, Pestalozzi, Froebel and Herbart read and were influenced by this work. The fundamental thesis of Rousseau was that a child was good by nature. Education must be child-centered. All learning must arise from a need felt by the child. The teacher must never exert any force in teaching. If a child is bad, it is because he learned this from an adult. A child is disciplined only through his suffering the consequences of his actions.

QUESTION 20.

Discuss the influence of Europe on American schools.

ANSWER.

The major European influence upon American education came from England. The framers of the Constitution did not place education under the control of the Federal government. The absence of any mention of education put it under the rule of each individual state. The ultimate responsibility for education rests with the parents. This position is consistent with *English tradition.*

However, *the Calvinist tradition* adopted in New England made education a state concern, led to universal education, and taxation of the community for the support of education. This tradition spread slowly to other areas of the newly-formed republic. The parochial nature of these schools began the tradition of *parochial education.* As new immigrants came with different faiths, more schools were attached to new religious parishes. The decision of the Supreme Court in the Oregon case, 1924, preserved the integrity of parochial education in the United States.

The dame school, the monitor school, the charity school, the workshop school and the Latin grammar school were important imports from England during the Colonial times. Early American colleges took their curriculum and organization from England.

During the nineteenth century many American educators traveled to Europe in order to study new ideas and improvements in education. The seventh Annual Report of *Horace Mann* described the educational systems in many European countries. His admiration of the Prussian schools, which were modeled upon Pestalozzian ideas, contributed to changes in American teaching. The *Normal School movement for the training of teachers* was imported from Europe. The movement for state-supported education was encouraged by European successes in this area.

QUESTION 21.

Discuss the Junior College Movement in the United States.

ANSWER.

Junior college is a two-year institution of higher learning. It offers a curriculum which prepares some students for transfer into the third year of college in another institution. It trains other students in semi-professional skills, completing the training within the two year course of study.

The first law providing for the establishment and support of a junior college was passed by the California Legislature in 1907. There were only ten of these public institutions in 1910. By 1950 over five hundred schools were in existence in most of the States. The largest numbers exist in California and in Michigan. The demand for skilled technicians, the need for more education beyond the secondary level and the growing problem of the cost of higher education lend impetus to the development of community-supported junior colleges. These colleges provide inexpensive higher education for those young men and women who must live at home.

QUESTION 22.

How did the infant school develop?

ANSWER.

The infant school was initiated by *Robert Owen* in Scotland in 1799. It was introduced into *Boston in 1816*. This school was the forerunner of the modern kindergarten. It admitted children who were four years of age. Owen's schools existed for children of the working poor. In the United States the school became a *part of the regular public school system* in Boston in 1818. The purpose was to provide a pleasant atmosphere, songs, games and nature study. This gave the child the social background to learn well in the elementary school. Such schools as these were the kindergartens founded by Froebel and introduced into the United States public school system in 1873 at St. Louis.

QUESTION 23.

What is the United States Office of Education?

ANSWER.

Henry Barnard publicized the need for a federal agency that would coordinate the educational progress of the various states and provide information to each of the states. Barnard won the support of the newly formed National Educational Association. Congress passed a law in 1867 creating the National Department of Education. It authorized the appointment of a Commissioner and a staff. Henry Barnard was named the first Commissioner. This department now is called the Office of Education. It is under the Department of Health, Education and Welfare.

QUESTION 24.

What is understood by "traditional education?"

ANSWER.

Traditional education describes the method of teaching which is *teacher-centered*. The curriculum is planned without any consideration of the present needs of the child. It emphasizes *what to think rather than how to think.* In the teaching act the child passively assimilates what he is told. There is little opportunity provided for movement, exploration and discovery. Although internal motivation might exist by accident, the usual motivation is the stressing of rewards and punishments for success and failure. The classroom atmosphere is more competitive than cooperative. The subject which is studied by the child is believed to be good both in itself and because it provides intellectual growth and self-discipline.

QUESTION 25.

What is understood by "progressive education?"

ANSWER.

Progressive education aims at *teaching the child how to think.* Material is provided to awaken his interest, stimulate his curiosity and achieve the internal motivation necessary for learning. Each child is considered as *an individual* who must proceed at his own pace upon the principle of readiness. He is not to be forced to learn. The learning is based upon his experience and nature, here and now. The learner must have a felt need for learning. The classroom is child-centered. The teacher guides and inspires the child.

BIBLIOGRAPHY OF PRIMARY SOURCES FOR THE STUDY OF THE HISTORY OF EDUCATION

Appendix 2

Alexander, Carter, *How to Locate Educational Information and Data.* New York, Columbia University Press, 1935.

Altekar, A.S., *Education in Ancient India.* Benares, Kishore, 1948.

Barnard, H.C., *A Short History of English Education from 1760 to 1944.* London, University of London Press, 1947.

Barnes, H.E., *A History of Historical Writing.* Norman, Univ. of Oklahoma, 1937.

Brickman, W.W., *A Guide to Research in Educational History.* New York, N.Y.U. Bookstore, 1949.

Brubacher, J.S., *A History of the Problems of Education.* New York, McGraw-Hill, 1947.

Butts, R.F., *A Cultural History of Education.* New York, McGraw-Hill, 1947.

Cremin, L.A. and Butts, R.F., *A History of Education in American Culture.* New York, Holt and Co., 1953.

Eby, F., *The Development of Modern Education: In Theory, Organization and Practice.* New York, Prentice-Hall, 1952.

Eby, F. and Arrowood, C.F., *The History and Philosophy of Education, Ancient and Medieval.* New York, Prentice-Hall, 1940.

Maritain, Jacques, *Three Reformers: Luther, Descartes, Rousseau.* New York, Scribners, 1929.

Meyer, A.E., *An Educational History of the American People.* New York, McGraw-Hill, 1957.

Meyer, A.E., *An Educational History of the Western World.* New York, McGraw-Hill, 1965.

Meyer, A.E., *The Development of Education in the Twentieth Century.* New York, Prentice-Hall, 1939.

Monroe, Paul, *Cyclopedia of Education.* 5 Vols. New York, Macmillan, 1911.

Monroe, Paul, *Encyclopaedia of Educational Research.* New York, Macmillan, 1950.

Monroe, W.S., *Comenius and Beginnings of Educational Reform.* New York, Scribner, 1900.

Monroe, W.S., *History of the Pestalozzian Movement in the United States.* Syracuse, Bardeen, 1907.

Monroe, W.S., *Teacher-Learning Theory and Teacher Education, 1890-1950.* Urbana, Univ. of Illinois Press, 1952.

Randall, J.H., *The Making of the Modern Mind.* Boston, Houghton Mifflin, 1940.

Rivlin, H. and Schueler, H.,(ed.), *Encyclopedia of Modern Education.* New York, Philosophical Library, 1943.

Thorndike, Lynn, *The History of Magic and Experimental Science.* 6 Vols. New York, Columbia University Press, 1923 through 1940.

Ulich, R., *Conditions of Civilized Living.* New York, E.P. Dutton, 1946.

Ulich, R., *History of Educational Thought.* New York, American Book, 1945.

Ulich, R., *Three Thousand Years of Educational Wisdom.* Cambridge, Mass., Harvard University Press, 1947.

Woody, Thomas, *Life and Education in Early Societies.* New York, Macmillan, 1949.

World Survey of Education: Handbook of Educational Organization and Statistics. New York, UNESCO, 1955.

MONARCH® NOTES AND STUDY GUIDES

...THE MOST COMPREHENSIVE SERIES OF STUDY GUIDES EVER PUBLISHED—

MONARCH NOTES AND STUDY GUIDES
MODERN ECONOMISTS

MONARCH® STUDY GUIDES

HIGH SCHOOL LEVEL

Size 8¹/₂"x11"— $1.25 to $1.50 Each

These comprehensive high school level review books are indispensable for every student. The book is 8¹/₂x11 in size ... and is composed of sheets that are perforated and easily removed from the book and inserted in the student's loose-leaf notebook. This provides the student with an up-to-the-minute summary of all material he is responsible for and allows him to organize his notes and study twice as effectively. By using this amazingly simple device the student can add his class notes to his review notes, thus forming a highly-organized set of notes when studying and following lectures by his teachers.

LANGUAGE

115-6	SPANISH—ONE YEAR NOTES
107-3	SPANISH—TWO YEARS NOTES
114-9	SPANISH—THREE YEARS NOTES
113-1	FRENCH—ONE YEAR NOTES
108-1	FRENCH—TWO YEARS NOTES ($1.50)
109-9	FRENCH—THREE YEARS NOTES ($1.50)
116-4	LATIN—ONE YEAR NOTES
117-2	LATIN—TWO YEARS NOTES
132-7	LATIN—THREE YEARS NOTES
128-9	GERMAN—ONE YEAR NOTES
129-7	GERMAN—TWO YEARS NOTES

ENGLISH

125-5	ENGLISH—TWO YEARS NOTES
106-5	ENGLISH—THREE YEARS NOTES
111-5	ENGLISH—4 YRS. NOTES ($1.50)

HISTORY

101-6	AMERICAN HISTORY NOTES
102-4	WORLD HISTORY NOTES ($1.50)
122-2	GEOGRAPHY NOTES ($1.50)
131-3	AMERICAN HISTORY AND WORLD BACKGROUNDS ($1.50)
133-9	AMERICAN GOVERNMENT ($1.50)
134-7	CITIZENSHIP EDUCATION (PRELIMINARY TO SOCIAL STUDIES) ($1.50)

SCIENCE

103-2	ELEMENTARY BIOLOGY NOTES
104-0	CHEMISTRY NOTES ($1.50)
105-7	PHYSICS NOTES
112-3	EARTH SCIENCE NOTES ($1.50)
124-8	GENERAL SCIENCE NOTES

MATHEMATICS

123-0	7th-8th GRADE MATH NOTES (WITH NEW MATH)
118-0	ELEMENTARY ALGEBRA NOTES (9th YEAR MATH)
119-8	INTERMEDIATE ALGEBRA NOTES (2nd YEAR ALGEBRA)
110-7	GEOMETRY NOTES (10th YEAR MATH) ($1.50)
121-4	11th YEAR MATH NOTES ($1.50)
120-6	TRIGONOMETRY NOTES
126-3	ADVANCED ALGEBRA (12A MATH) ($1.50)

ECONOMICS & BUSINESS

127-1	BUSINESS ARITHMETIC
135-4	BOOKKEEPING

MONARCH NOTES AND STUDY GUIDES
HIGH SCHOOL LEVEL
BIOLOGY

MONARCH® NOTES AND STUDY GUIDES
HIGH SCHOOL LEVEL
ELEMENTARY ALGEBRA
(9th YEAR MATH)

COLLEGE LEVEL

Size 8¹/₂"x 11" **$1.95 to $2.50 Each**

Designed for a quick but comprehensive review of all coursework. These books have been carefully researched specifically to cover the curriculum at the college level. All essential information is simply and clearly explained. All obscure points are clarified to help the reader derive the greatest possible benefit. These books will give the student a powerful command of the subject. Each book contains sample exam questions and answers to test the reader's grasp of the subject.

HISTORY & GOVERNMENT

9000-1	WORLD HISTORY, PART 1 (Western Civilization) ($1.95)
9020-9	WORLD HISTORY, PART 2 (Western Civilization) ($1.95)
9040-7	AMERICAN GOVERNMENT ($2.25)
9050-6	AMERICAN HISTORY TO 1865 ($1.95)
9060-5	AMERICAN HIST. FROM 1865 ($1.95)
9070-4	MEDIEVAL HISTORY ($1.95)
9080-3	CONTEMPORARY CIVILIZATION PART 1 ($2.50)
9090-2	CONTEMPORARY CIVILIZATION PART 2 ($2.50)
9100-9	PHILOSOPHY ($2.25)
9110-8	ANCIENT HISTORY ($2.25)
9120-7	HISTORY OF ENGLAND ($2.25)
9130-6	HISTORY OF RUSSIA ($2.25)
9140-5	WORLD HISTORY SINCE 1914 ($2.25)
9150-4	COMPARATIVE GOVERNMENT ($2.25)
9500-0	DIPLOMATIC HISTORY OF THE UNITED STATES ($2.25)
9510-9	ASIAN CIVILIZATION ($2.25)
9520-8	POLITICAL SCIENCE (Government and the Political Process) ($2.25)
9530-7	INTERNATIONAL AFFAIRS AND WORLD POLITICS ($2.25)

ECONOMICS & BUSINESS

9160-3	ECONOMICS ($1.95)
9170-2	MARKETING ($2.25)
9180-1	INTRODUCTORY ACCT'G. ($2.25)
9190-0	SECURITIES & INVESTMENTS ($2.25)
9200-7	CORPORATE FINANCE ($2.25)
9210-6	MONEY AND BANKING ($2.25)
9220-5	BUSINESS MANAGEMENT ($2.25)
9230-4	BUSINESS LAW ($2.25)
9550-5	ECONOMIC HISTORY OF THE UNITED STATES ($2.25)
9560-4	LABOR ECONOMICS ($2.25)
9570-3	INSURANCE ($2.25)
9590-1	SALES MANAGEMENT ($2.25)
9680-0	ELEMENTS OF BUSINESS ($2.25)

SCIENCE & MATHEMATICS

9240-3	BIOLOGY ($1.95)
9250-2	ZOOLOGY ($2.25)
9260-1	BOTANY ($1.95)
9270-0	CHEMISTRY, PART 1 WITH SOLVED PROBLEMS ($1.95)
9280-9	CHEMISTRY, PART 2 WITH SOLVED PROBLEMS ($1.95)
9290-8	COLLEGE GEOLOGY ($2.25)
9300-5	PHYSICAL SCIENCE (EARTH SCIENCE) ($2.25)
9310-4	COLLEGE GEOGRAPHY ($2.25)
9320-3	STATISTICS ($2.25)
9600-8	GEOLOGY LAB MANUAL ($2.50)
9610-7	PHYSICS LAB MANUAL ($2.50)

PSYCHOLOGY, SOCIOLOGY AND EDUCATION

9330-2	PSYCHOLOGY ($1.95)
9340-1	SOCIOLOGY ($1.95)
9350-0	CHILD PSYCHOLOGY ($1.95)
9370-8	EDUCATIONAL PSYCH. ($1.95)
9380-7	ANTHROPOLOGY ($2.25)
9630-5	HIST. OF EDUCATION ($2.25)
9360-9	PHIL. OF EDUCATION ($2.25)
9640-4	THE PRINCIPLES OF CONTEMPORARY EDUCATION ($2.25)
9690-9	PSYCHOLOGICAL TESTING ($2.25)

ART AND MUSIC

9400-3	ART HISTORY ($2.25)
9390-6	HISTORY OF MUSIC ($2.25)
9410-2	INTRO. TO MUSIC ($2.25)

ENGLISH & LANGUAGE

9420-1	REVIEW OF BASIC ENGLISH GRAMMAR FOR COLLEGE STUDENTS ($1.95)
9430-0	SPANISH GRAMMAR— COLLEGE LEVEL ($2.25)
9440-9	FRENCH GRAMMAR— COLLEGE LEVEL ($2.25)
9650-3	GERMAN GRAMMAR— COLLEGE LEVEL ($2.25)
9450-8	SPEECH ($1.95)
9660-2	PUBLIC SPEAKING ($1.95)
9670-1	INTRO. TO JOURNALISM ($2.25)

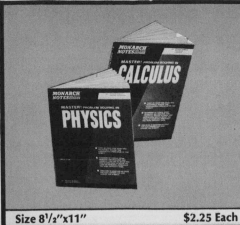

MONARCH LITERATURE STUDY GUIDES

826-8	EARLY CHURCH FATHERS— The Writings ($1.50)	839-1	HEMINGWAY—Snows of Kilimanjaro	677-5	JAMES—The Ambassadors	622-1	MAUGHAM—Of Human Bondage

EARLY CHURCH FATHERS—The Writings ($1.50) — 826-8

- 707-0 EIGHTEENTH-CENTURY RESTORATION PLAYS ($1.95)
- 708-8 ELIOT—Adam Bede
- 709-6 ELIOT—Middlemarch
- 710-4 ELIOT—Mill on the Floss
- 612-2 ELIOT—Silas Marner
- 782-1 ELIOT, T. S.—Murder in the Cathedral & Selected Poems
- 663-5 EMERSON—The Writings
- 829-2 EURIPIDES—The Plays
- 508-2 EURIPIDES, AESCHYLUS & ARISTOPHANES—The Plays
- 830-0 EUROPEAN LITERATURE— Part 1 ($1.95)

- 664-3 FAULKNER—Absalom, Absalom!
- 665-0 FAULKNER—As I Lay Dying
- 666-8 FAULKNER—Light in August
- 613-0 FAULKNER—The Sound and the Fury & other novels
- 559-5 FEDERALIST PAPERS
- 711-2 FIELDING—Joseph Andrews
- 614-8 FIELDING—Tom Jones
- 667-6 FITZGERALD—The Great Gatsby
- 668-4 FITZGERALD—Tender is the Night
- 560-3 FLAUBERT—Madame Bovary and The Three Tales
- 831-8 FORBES—Johnny Tremain
- 712-0 FORSTER—Passage to India & Howards End
- 561-1 FRANK—Diary of a Young Girl
- 832-6 FRANKLIN—Autobiography
- 833-4 FRENCH LITERATURE ($1.95)
- 615-5 FREUD—On His Writings and Ideas
- 783-1 FROST—The Poems

- 835-9 GIDE—The Immoralist and Strait Is the Gate
- 521-5 GOETHE—Faust
- 836-7 GOETHE—Sorrows of Young Werther
- 893-8 GOLDING—The Inheritors and Free Fall
- 616-3 GOLDING—Lord of the Flies
- 892-0 GOLDING—Pincher Martin
- 837-5 GOLDSMITH—She Stoops to Conquer and other works
- 755-9 GOLDSMITH—Vicar of Wakefield
- 500-9 GREEK AND ROMAN CLASSICS ($2.25)
- 838-3 GREENE—The Major Novels (Power and the Glory, Brighton Rock, Heart of the Matter and others)

- 669-2 HALE—Man Without a Country
- 890-4 HARDY—Far from the Madding Crowd
- 713-8 HARDY—Jude the Obscure
- 617-1 HARDY—Mayor of Casterbridge
- 618-9 HARDY—Return of the Native
- 619-7 HARDY—Tess of the D'Urbervilles
- 670-6 HAWTHORNE—House of Seven Gables & Marble Faun
- 620-5 HAWTHORNE—The Scarlet Letter
- 528-0 HEGEL—The Philosophy
- 621-3 HEMINGWAY—The Major Novels
- 671-8 HEMINGWAY—Farewell to Arms
- 672-6 HEMINGWAY—For Whom the Bell Tolls
- 673-4 HEMINGWAY—The Old Man and the Sea

- 839-1 HEMINGWAY—Snows of Kilimanjaro
- 674-2 HEMINGWAY—The Sun Also Rises
- 503-3 HERODOTUS—The Persian Wars
- 840-9 HERSEY—Bell for Adano, Hiroshima and other works
- 841-7 HEYERDAHL—Kon-Tiki and Aku-Aku
- 842-5 HILTON—Goodbye, Mr. Chips and Lost Horizon
- 896-1 HITLER—Concise Biography
- 501-7 HOMER—Iliad
- 502-5 HOMER—Odyssey
- 784-9 HOPKINS—The Poems
- 885-4 HOW TO ANALYZE DRAMA ($1.50)
- 886-2 HOW TO ANALYZE FICTION ($1.50)
- 887-0 HOW TO ANALYZE POETRY ($1.50)
- 834-2 HOW TO WRITE THEMES ($1.50)
- 888-8 HOW TO WRITE THESES ($1.50)
- 675-9 HOWELLS—Rise of Silas Lapham
- 844-1 HUGO—Les Miserables
- 529-8 HUME—The Philosophy
- 714-6 HUXLEY—The Major Novels (Brave New World, Point Counterpoint and others)

- 562-9 IBSEN—The Major Plays
- 676-7 IRVING—Legend of Sleepy Hollow

MONARCH NOTES and STUDY GUIDES — MELVILLE'S MOBY DICK — PRICE $1.00

- 677-5 JAMES—The Ambassadors
- 678-3 JAMES—The American
- 845-8 JAMES—The Aspern Papers
- 679-1 JAMES—Portrait of a Lady
- 680-9 JAMES—Turn of the Screw & Daisy Miller
- 846-6 JAMES—Washington Square
- 563-7 JOYCE—Portrait of the Artist as a Young Man & Dubliners
- 564-5 JOYCE—Ulysses

- 847-4 KAFKA—The Trial, The Castle and other works
- 530-6 KANT—The Philosophy
- 785-6 KEATS—The Poems
- 715-3 KIPLING—Captains Courageous & other works
- 848-2 KIPLING—Kim and The Jungle Books
- 889-6 KNOWLES—A Separate Peace
- 849-0 KOESTLER—Darkness at Noon

- 716-1 LAWRENCE—Sons and Lovers & other works
- 681-7 LEE—To Kill a Mockingbird
- 682-5 LEWIS—Arrowsmith
- 683-3 LEWIS—Babbitt
- 004-1 LEWIS—Main Street
- 531-4 LOCKE AND HOBBES— The Philosophies
- 850-8 LOGIC—Deductive ($1.50)
- 685-8 LONDON—Call of the Wild
- 786-4 LONGFELLOW—Evangeline & other poems

- 565-2 MACHIAVELLI—The Prince
- 566-0 MANN—The Major Works
- 717-9 MARLOWE—Dr. Faustus and other works
- 544-7 MARXIST & UTOPIAN SOCIALISTS (Marx, Engels, Owen, Lenin, & others)
- 851-6 MAUGHAM—Moon and Sixpence and Razor's Edge

- 622-1 MAUGHAM—Of Human Bondage
- 686-6 MELVILLE—Billy Budd
- 623-9 MELVILLE—Moby Dick and other works
- 852-4 MEREDITH—The Ordeal of Richard Feverel
- 532-2 MILL, BENTHAM AND THE UTILITARIAN SCHOOL
- 687-4 MILLER—The Crucible and View From the Bridge
- 688-2 MILLER—Death of a Salesman
- 513-2 MILTON—Paradise Lost and other works
- 787-2 MILTON—The Poems (exclusive of Paradise Lost)
- 854-0 MODERN AMERICAN DRAMA ($1.95)
- 624-7 MODERN BRITISH AND IRISH DRAMA
- 533-0 MODERN ECONOMISTS (George, Keynes, Hayek, Schumpeter, Galbraith and others)
- 567-8 MODERN EUROPEAN DRAMA
- 568-6 MOLIERE—The Plays
- 855-7 MONTAIGNE—Essays of
- 856-5 MORE—Utopia
- 895-3 MUSSOLINI—Concise Biography
- 523-1 MYTHOLOGY

- 625-4 NEW TESTAMENT ($1.50)
- 534-8 NIETZSCHE— The Major Works
- 535-5 NINETEENTH-CENTURY SOCIOLOGISTS (Durkheim, Comte, Spencer, Weber and others)
- 857-3 NORDHOFF & HALL— Mutiny on the Bounty
- 891-2 NORRIS—The Octopus

- 626-8 OLD TESTAMENT ($1.50)
- 627-0 O'NEILL—The Major Plays
- 750-0 O'NEILL—Desire Under the Elms
- 751-8 O'NEILL—Iceman Cometh
- 752-6 O'NEILL—Long Day's Journey into Night

GREAT IDEA SERIES

SERIES SHOWN HERE FOR REFERENCE ONLY.
TITLES IN ALPHABETICAL LISTS ABOVE AND ON OTHER PAGES

Philosophers and Political Philosophers

- AMERICAN POLITICAL PHILOSOPHY
- ARISTOTLE—The Philosophy ($1.50)
- BERKELEY—The Philosophy
- COMMUNIST THEORY FROM MARX TO MAO, OUTLINE & CRITICISM OF ($1.50)
- CONSTITUTION—Leading Cases ($1.95)
- DARWIN AND SPENCER
- DESCARTES—The Philosophy
- EARLY CHURCH FATHERS— The Writings ($1.50)
- FEDERALIST PAPERS
- FREUD—On His Writings and Ideas
- HEGEL—The Philosophy
- HUME—The Philosophy

- KANT—The Philosophy
- LOCKE AND HOBBES— The Philosophies
- LOGIC—Deductive ($1.50)
- MILL, BENTHAM AND THE UTILITARIAN SCHOOL
- NIETZSCHE—The Major Works
- PLATO—The Republic and Selected Dialogues
- ROUSSEAU AND THE 18TH-CENTURY POLITICAL PHILOSOPHERS
- RUSSELL—The Philosophy
- ST. THOMAS AQUINAS— The Philosophy
- ST. AUGUSTINE—The Works
- SCHOPENHAUER—The Philosophy
- SCIENCE—The Philosophy of ($1.95)
- SPINOZA—The Philosophy
- TWENTIETH-CENTURY FASCISM
- 20th CENTURY PHILOSOPHERS

- UNITED NATIONS ($1.95)
- VOLTAIRE—Candide (and the Philosophes)

Economists

- CLASSICAL ECONOMISTS (Smith, Ricardo and Malthus)
- MARXIST & UTOPIAN SOCIALISTS (Marx, Engels, Owen, Lenin, & others)
- MODERN ECONOMISTS (George, Keynes, Hayek, Schumpeter, Galbraith & others)

Sociology & Education

- NINETEENTH-CENTURY SOCIOLOGISTS (Durkheim, Comte, Spencer, Weber & others)
- 20TH-CENTURY EDUCATORS
- TWENTIETH-CENTURY SOCIOLOGISTS (Lerner, Riesman, and many others)

MONARCH LITERATURE STUDY GUIDES

753-4	O'NEILL—Mourning Becomes Electra
754-2	O'NEILL—Strange Interlude
718-7	ORWELL—Animal Farm
719-5	ORWELL—1984
720-3	PATON—Cry, the Beloved Country & Too Late the Phalarope
505-8	PLATO—The Republic and Selected Dialogues
689-0	POE—Tales and Poems
788-0	POPE—Rape of the Lock and other poems
789-8	POUND—The Poems
735-1	PRE-TWENTIETH CENTURY AMERICAN POETS, SURVEY OF
858-1	RACINE AND CORNEILLE— The Plays
859-9	RAWLINGS—The Yearling
861-5	REMARQUE—All Quiet on the Western Front
862-3	RICHTER—Light in the Forest and The Sea of Grass
860-7	RIESMAN—The Lonely Crowd
690-8	ROLVAAG—Giants in the Earth
518-1	ROMANTIC POETS, SURVEY OF (Byron, Shelley, Keats & many others) ($1.95)
865-6	ROMAN LITERATURE ($1.95)
863-1	ROSTAND—Cyrano de Bergerac
536-3	ROUSSEAU AND THE 18TH-CENTURY POLITICAL PHILOSOPHERS
864-9	RUSSELL—The Philosophy
546-2	ST. THOMAS AQUINAS— The Philosophy
537-1	ST. AUGUSTINE—The Works
691-6	SALINGER—The Catcher in the Rye
866-4	SALINGER—Franny and Zooey and Nine Stories
867-2	SANDBURG—Lincoln, The Prairie Years
569-4	SARTRE—No Exit, The Flies and other works
538-9	SCHOPENHAUER—The Philosophy
868-0	SCIENCE–The Philosophy of ($1.95)
628-8	SCOTT—Ivanhoe & other works

SHAKESPEARE SERIES

869-8	SHAKESPEARE—All's Well That Ends Well
630-4	SHAKESPEARE—Antony and Cleopatra
631-2	SHAKESPEARE—As You Like It
870-6	SHAKESPEARE—Comedy of Errors
652-8	SHAKESPEARE—Coriolanus
514-0	SHAKESPEARE—Hamlet
632-0	SHAKESPEARE—Julius Caesar
633-8	SHAKESPEARE—Henry IV, Part 1
634-6	SHAKESPEARE—Henry IV, Part 2
635-3	SHAKESPEARE—Henry V
515-7	SHAKESPEARE—King Lear
516-5	SHAKESPEARE—Macbeth
636-1	SHAKESPEARE—Measure for Measure
637-9	SHAKESPEARE—Merchant of Venice
638-7	SHAKESPEARE—Midsummer Night's Dream
639-5	SHAKESPEARE—Much Ado About Nothing
640-3	SHAKESPEARE—Othello
641-1	SHAKESPEARE—Richard II
642-9	SHAKESPEARE—Richard III
643-7	SHAKESPEARE—Romeo and Juliet
653-6	SHAKESPEARE—Sonnets
654-4	SHAKESPEARE—Taming of the Shrew
644-5	SHAKESPEARE—The Tempest
655-1	SHAKESPEARE—Troilus and Cressida & other selected tragedies
645-2	SHAKESPEARE—Twelfth Night
871-4	SHAKESPEARE—Two Gentlemen of Verona
656-9	SHAKESPEARE—The Winter's Tale
629-6	SHAKESPEARE—Selected Comedies including: All's Well That Ends Well, Taming of the Shrew, The Winter's Tale, The Comedy of Errors, Two Gentlemen of Verona, The Merry Wives of Windsor, & Love's Labour's Lost
646-0	SHAW—Major Plays
872-2	SHAW—Arms and the Man
721-1	SHAW—Caesar and Cleopatra
873-0	SHAW—Candida

722-9	SHAW—Major Barbara
723-7	SHAW—Man and Superman
724-5	SHAW—Pygmalion
725-2	SHAW—Saint Joan
732-8	SHELLEY—The Poems
874-8	SHERWOOD—Abe Lincoln in Illinois
507-4	SOPHOCLES—The Plays
512-4	SPENSER—The Faerie Queene and other works
539-7	SPINOZA—The Philosophy
647-8	STEINBECK—The Major Novels
692-4	STEINBECK—Grapes of Wrath
693-2	STEINBECK—Of Mice and Men
694-0	STEINBECK—The Red Pony and The Pearl
570-2	STENDHAL—Red and the Black & Charterhouse of Parma
875-5	STERNE—Tristram Shandy
790-6	STEVENS, WALLACE—The Poems
876-3	STEVENSON—Kidnapped
726-0	STEVENSON—Treasure Island
648-6	SWIFT—Gulliver's Travels
734-4	TENNYSON—Idylls of the King & other poems
727-8	THACKERAY—Vanity Fair and Henry Esmond
730-2	THOMAS, DYLAN—The Poems
695-7	THOREAU—Walden and other writings
504-1	THUCYDIDES—Peloponnesian Wars

571-0	TOLSTOY—Anna Karenina
572-8	TOLSTOY—War and Peace
894-6	TRUMAN—Concise Biography
877-1	TURGENEV—Fathers and Sons
879-7	TWAIN—Connecticut Yankee and others
649-4	TWAIN—Huckleberry Finn and other novels
878-9	TWAIN—Prince and the Pauper
696-5	TWAIN—Tom Sawyer
520-7	TWENTIETH-CENTURY BRITISH AND AMERICAN POETS, SURVEY OF
540-5	20TH-CENTURY EDUCATORS
541-3	TWENTIETH-CENTURY FASCISM
542-1	TWENTIETH-CENTURY PHILOSOPHERS
543-9	TWENTIETH-CENTURY SOCIOLOGISTS (Lerner, Riesman, and many others)
880-5	UNITED NATIONS ($1.95)
519-9	VICTORIAN POETS, SURVEY OF (Arnold, Browning, Tennyson & many others)
509-0	VIRGIL—The Aeneid & other works
545-4	VOLTAIRE—Candide (and the Philosophes)
697-3	WARREN—All the King's Men
698-1	WHARTON—Ethan Frome
736-9	WHITMAN—Leaves of Grass
881-3	WILDE, OSCAR—The Plays
699-9	WILDER—Our Town, Bridge of San Luis Rey & other works
650-2	WILLIAMS—Major Plays
700-5	WILLIAMS—Glass Menagerie
701-3	WILLIAMS—Streetcar Named Desire
737-7	WILLIAMS, W. C.—The Poems
882-1	WISTER—The Virginian
702-1	WOLFE—Look Homeward, Angel & Of Time and the River
703-9	WOLFE—You Can't Go Home Again & The Web and the Rock
883-9	WOOLF—Mrs. Dalloway, and To the Lighthouse
729-4	WORDSWORTH—The Poems
738-5	YEATS—The Poems

POETRY SERIES

SERIES SHOWN HERE FOR REFERENCE ONLY.
TITLES IN ALPHABETICAL LISTS ABOVE AND ON OTHER PAGES

AUDEN, W. H.—The Poems	FROST—The Poems	SHELLEY—The Poems
ARNOLD—The Poems	HOPKINS—The Poems	STEVENS, WALLACE—The Poems
BLAKE—The Poems	HOW TO ANALYZE POETRY ($1.50)	TENNYSON—Idylls of the King & other poems
BROWNING, ROBERT—The Poems	KEATS—The Poems	THOMAS, DYLAN—The Poems
COLERIDGE—Ancient Mariner, Kubla Khan & other poems	LONGFELLOW—Evangeline & other poems	TWENTIETH-CENTURY BRITISH AND AMERICAN POETS, SURVEY OF
CRANE, HART—The Poems	MILTON—The Poems (exclusive of Paradise Lost)	VICTORIAN POETS, SURVEY OF (Arnold, Browning, Tennyson & many others)
CUMMINGS—The Poems	POPE—Rape of the Lock & other poems	WHITMAN—Leaves of Grass
DICKINSON—The Poems	POUND—The Poems	WILLIAMS, W. C.—The Poems
DONNE—The Poems & the Metaphysical poets	PRE-TWENTIETH CENTURY AMERICAN POETS, SURVEY OF	WORDSWORTH—The Poems
DRYDEN—The Poems	ROMANTIC POETS, SURVEY OF (Byron, Shelley, Keats & many others) ($1.95)	YEATS—The Poems
ELIOT, T. S.—Murder in the Cathedral and Selected Poems